WOVEN SPLENDOR

*Five Centuries of European Tapestry
in the Detroit Institute of Arts*

•

ALAN PHIPPS DARR
and
TRACEY ALBAINY
with
MELANIE HOLCOMB

D1591415

•

THE DETROIT INSTITUTE OF ARTS

•

This catalogue is published in conjunction with the exhibition
"Woven Splendor: Five Centuries of European Tapestry
in the Detroit Institute of Arts"
at the Detroit Institute of Arts, July 14–September 29, 1996.

•

This exhibition is sponsored by
Cadillac and the Metropolitan Detroit Cadillac Dealers
and is supported by the Founders Junior Council,
the William R. Hearst Foundation,
the John S. and James L. Knight Foundation,
and the National Endowment for the Arts.
The exhibition is also made possible with the support of
the Michigan Council for Arts and Cultural Affairs
and the Detroit Institute of Arts Founders Society.

•

•

Distributed by The University of Washington Press, Seattle and London

•

ISBN: 0-8143-2674-9

•

Library of Congress Cataloging-in-Publication Data:

Detroit Institute of Arts
    Woven splendor: five centuries of European tapestry in the Detroit Insti-
tute of Arts / Tracey Albainy and Alan Phipps Darr with Melanie Holcomb.
        p.   cm.
    Exhibition catalog.
    Includes bibliographical references and index.
    ISBN 0-8143-2674-9
    1. Tapestry—Europe—Exhibitions. 2. Tapestry—Michigan—Detroit—
Exhibitions. 3. Detroit Institute of Arts—Exhibitions.
    I. Albainy, Tracey. II. Darr, Alan Phipps. III. Holcomb, Melanie.
NK3042.D48 1996
746.394'074'77434—dc20   96-28582
                                                         CIP

COVER: Detail from *Winter,* CAT. NO. 13

TABLE OF CONTENTS

•

FOREWORD

erhaps there is no better example of the dilemma facing a museum, torn between concerns for the preservation of fragile works of art and the desire to exhibit them, than tapestries. These resplendent fabrics are woven of yarns that are inherently fugitive in color and, like watercolors, exposure to light begins a fading process that is irreversible. But what purpose is there in owning world-class treasures if you can never display them? Thus we have chosen to take the conservative middle road and display the greatest of our tapestry holdings in "Woven Splendor," but only for a short time and under carefully controlled conditions. Many of the tapestries exhibited have been recently cleaned and restored and it is a great pleasure for us all to see them in a state approaching their original magnificence. European tapestries were extremely expensive works of art to produce and were owned by only the wealthiest individuals in society but here they are made available for all of us to enjoy.

Detail from *Shepherd and Shepherdess* (CAT. NO. 2)

The exhibition of twenty tapestries features only a fraction of the museum's holdings in this medium, but they represent a cross-section of the most significant weaving centers, important design traditions, and decorative applications in western Europe from about 1500 until the early twentieth century. We hope that the enjoyment of these large, colorful, and richly detailed works of art will delight museum visitors and increase awareness of the many treasures in our museum's textiles collection, which must perforce be carefully stored away most of the time.

The co-curators of this exhibition, Alan P. Darr and Tracey Albainy, both of the department of European Sculpture and Decorative Arts, have ably handled the myriad details of its organization. Over the years they have received invaluable assistance from many textile specialists. Much of the current knowledge on the collection derives from the scholarly contributions made by Adolfo S. Cavallo and Edith A. Standen, both formerly of the Metropolitan Museum of Art, New York. Cavallo began his professional career at the Detroit Institute of Arts in 1954 and later returned as a curatorial consultant for textiles in 1978. In 1984, with funds provided by a National Endowment for the Arts Visiting Scholars grant, Standen studied and wrote lengthy notes on the post-medieval tapestries. Our debt to both of them is enormous.

Other specialists have generously assisted with research and preparation of the exhibition: in France, Daniel Alcouffe, Susanne Cussell, Nicole de Pazzis-Chevalier, Dominique Chevalier, Laurence de Lamaïstre, Amaury Lefébure, Hervé Oursel, and Philippe Palasi; in Belgium, Guy Delmarcel, Yvan Maes, and An Volckaert; in Great Britain, Patricia Collins, the S. Franses Tapestry Research Archives, Wendy Hefford, and Linda Parry; and in the United States, Candace Adelson, Sanford and Helen Berger, Charissa Bremer-David, Onica Busuioceanu, Thomas Campbell, Mark Coir, Theodore Dell, Marlene Eidelheit, Henry Hawley, the late Bruce Hutchinson, Gerhardt Knodel, Tracey Schuster, Karen Serota, Christa Mayer Thurman, Janet Whitson and the staff at the Rare Book Room of the Detroit Public Library, and Alice Zriebec. Special thanks go to Philippe Palasi, who identified the heraldic devices, and especially to Nicole de Pazzis-Chevalier, Guy Delmarcel, and Thomas Campbell, whose correspondence and conversations with the curators led to many new discoveries and a deeper understanding of the art of tapestry.

To enhance the presentation of *The Passing of Venus* tapestry, the exhibition includes the Burne-Jones gouache sketch for the cartoon, on loan from the Metropolitan Museum of Art, and a second Merton Abbey tapestry,

David Instructing Solomon on the Building of the Temple, also designed by Burne-Jones and lent by Christ Church, Cranbrook, in Bloomfield Hills, Michigan. We are grateful to George Goldner and Perrin Stein, Department of Drawings and Prints, the Metropolitan Museum of Art, and to Kathy Doyle, Parish Administrator, Christ Church, Cranbrook, for supporting and arranging these loans.

Nearly all the tapestries in this exhibition have been conserved over the last fifteen years under the direction of Barbara Heller, head of the museum's Conservation Services Laboratory. Many tapestries were treated in the museum's textile laboratory by textile conservators Jane Hutchins and Rita Kauneckas. Hutchins also advised on the selection of works and mechanics of the gallery installation. We are also grateful to the Textile Conservation Laboratory, Cathedral Church of Saint John the Divine, New York, and to Chevalier Conservation in France for their assistance.

Detail from *The Animal Tamers* (CAT. NO. 15)

This exhibition could only have been realized with the collaboration of many colleagues in the museum. In the European Sculpture and Decorative Arts department, the encouragement, patience, and assistance of Peter Barnet, Anna Jolly, and Lois Makee must be acknowledged. Melanie Holcomb capably assumed a major role in the preparation of the catalogue text and the didactic materials in the exhibition. Becky Hart, intern in the Twentieth Century department, also offered many useful suggestions.

Louis Gauci, Director of Exhibitions and Design, developed a thoughtful installation scheme, in the process overcoming several design obstacles. Jennifer Williams and Gina Granger, assistant curators in the Education department, scheduled a lively and varied program of public lectures and workshops. Ann Schumacher graciously lent a high-warp loom to be used for the weaving demonstration in the galleries. We are especially grateful to Mollie Fletcher for her advice on the many practical details of the demonstration; she also created an original cartoon to be woven.

The excellent photography was produced by Dirk Bakker, Director of Photography, and Robert Hensleigh, Associate Director, assisted by Eric Wheeler. The attractive catalogue design is the work of Don Hammond. The map of tapestry centers was created for the catalogue with the assistance of Ari Kambouris of the Exhibition Coordination department. Julia Henshaw, Director of Publications, edited the catalogue and coordinated its production with the help of Maria Santangelo, Editorial Assistant. This catalogue will provide a useful record of the tapestry collection for many years to come.

For their important roles in coordinating loans, shipment for conservation treatment, installation, fund raising, and publicity, we gratefully acknowledge Pamela Watson, Kimberly Dzuirman, Paul Smith, Terry Birkett, Michael Kociemba, and others in the Registrar's office; John McDonagh and James Huntley in the Development department; and Cyndi Summers, Pamela Phillips, and Laura Arnsbarger in the Marketing and Public Relations department.

Finally, this exhibition would not have been possible without the generous funding provided by Cadillac and the Metropolitan Detroit Cadillac Dealers, the Founders Junior Council, The William R. Hearst Foundation, the John S. and James L. Knight Foundation, the National Endowment for the Arts, the Michigan Council for Arts and Cultural Affairs, and the Detroit Institute of Arts Founders Society.

↜❋↝

SAMUEL SACHS II, DIRECTOR

FIG. 1 Detail from *Triumph of Spring* (CAT. NO. 10)

"THE NOBLEST OF THE WEAVING ARTS"

European Tapestries in the Detroit Institute of Arts

ALAN PHIPPS DARR, CURATOR OF EUROPEAN SCULPTURE AND DECORATIVE ARTS

O ver a century ago William Morris, the designer and leader of the Arts and Crafts movement in England, advocated the revival of medieval and Renaissance tapestry weaving traditions used from the late fourteenth through the sixteenth centuries. He spoke for a return to a process in which artists designed their own tapestries and produced them on hand-operated looms, thereby abandoning the mechanical copying of paintings and engravings and the use of industrial machines prevalent at tapestry manufactories in England and France in the nineteenth century (London 1996: 40, 228–32). Morris's philosophy passionately urging the creation of hand-made textiles, furniture, ceramics, and metalwork was embraced in Europe and America. In the early twentieth century, southeastern Michigan became a center for the collecting and appreciation of tapestries and textiles. Morris's revival of traditional weaving helped inspire museum patrons and professionals earlier this century to establish and develop the collection of seventy-five European tapestries at the Detroit Institute of Arts, considered among the most significant such collections in the United States.

The museum's tapestries, ranging in date from the late fifteenth to the early twentieth centuries, represent most major European weaving centers and factories. Scholars such as J. P. Asselberghs, the Flemish tapestry specialist, have noted the importance of the Detroit collection. He observed that among the museum's "most beautiful" collections of Flemish art, "the tapestries there assume evidently a considerable significance" (Asselberghs 1974: 23). Over the past two decades the tapestry collection has been the focus of a series of curatorial and conservation campaigns to analyze, wash, and conserve some of the most important examples. This exhibition celebrates the rich international tradition of five centuries of European tapestry, reintroduces the distinguished collection of the Detroit Institute of Arts, and presents the first catalogue on the collection.

The term "tapestry" refers to a specific weaving technique. **Tapestry** is defined by its distinctive structure — a **weft**-faced plain weave with a discontinuous weft. Tapestry has ancient origins; examples with this same type of construction have been found from ancient China to the Near East, from Egypt to Peru, and in America from 1500 B.C. onward. Mastering this weaving technique to create a large luxury textile is a lengthy, highly specialized process.

The tapestry weave is a variant of the simple plain weave. In the plain weave the loom is prepared with one **warp** system. The weavers then add the weft perpendicular to the warp, going under one warp and over the next, across the width of the loom and reversing the sequence on the return. In the tapestry weave, the weft threads interface regularly with the warps as in a plain weave; however, with tapestry weave the weft threads, which are generally dyed various colors, do not span the width of the cloth but form the design by turning back on themselves when a change of color is needed; consequently they are discontinuous across the width of the loom. The wefts alone are used for design, color, and texture. To develop pattern and image, weavers of tapestries use more weft threads than warp threads to the inch. Since the colored weft does not span the width of the fabric, one of three methods of joining weft threads is used when two colors meet. By dovetailing two different wefts around a single warp thread, by interlocking the wefts with each other, or by returning the weft on itself, the colored wefts create the pattern and form the fabric . The colored weft

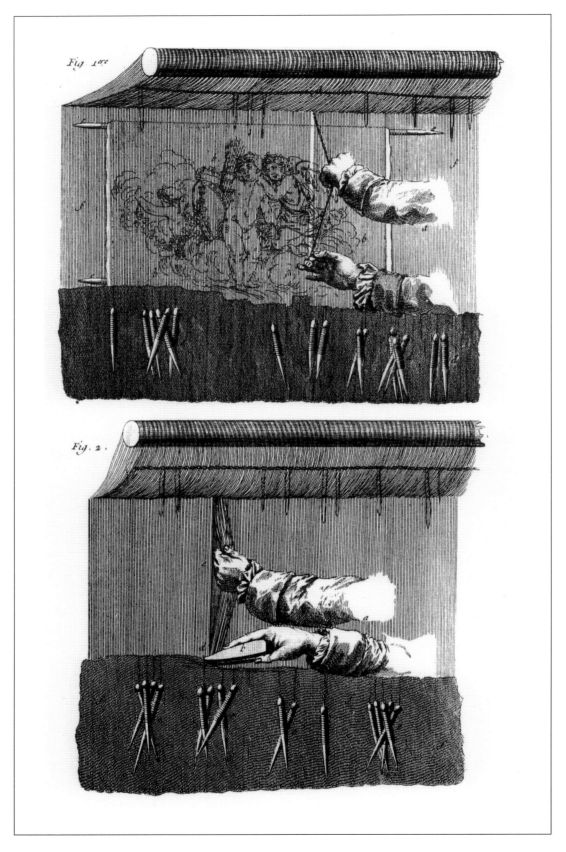

FIG. 2 The weaver's perspective from the back of a high-warp loom. At top, the weaver uses black chalk to mark the outlines for the tapestry design onto the individual warp threads. Suspended from a rod behind the warps is a tracing of the cartoon which the weaver uses as a guide. Below, a weaver uses a comb to press the wefts together to form the web of the cloth. (Diderot 1771)

threads are inserted loosely, then packed down firmly to cover the warps, which become the invisible support structure for the fabric whose design is the same on back and front.

Although tapestry-woven textiles have been used in the Near East, South America, and Asia to make tents, bedspreads, and other functional furnishings for centuries, the term "tapestry" is most often understood now as the type of wall or upholstery covering which has adorned castles and churches, courts and courtyards, especially in Europe north of the Alps since the late fourteenth and fifteenth centuries. Tapestry, woven either on a **high-warp** or **low-warp loom** (FIGS. 3, 4) usually from wool, linen and/or silk, as well as occasionally of gold or silver thread, has been heralded as "queen of all the crafts [which] reached its zenith in the pictorial hangings, woven in several countries of Europe from the late Middle Ages to the eighteenth century." The author of this quotation, Adele Coulin Weibel, the Detroit Institute of Arts's first curator of textiles (1927–49; curator emerita until 1963), organized the museum's last major tapestry exhibition in 1945.

By the fifteenth century, the industry and art of tapestry production in Europe was international. An outgrowth from the extensive cloth industry of medieval Europe, the production of tapestries depended on a regular supply of high-quality, finely spun wool. This often was imported from England, whose sheep were preferred for the strength, luster, and durability of their wool (Bennett 1992: 19). The short distance between London and Bruges, then the leading port city of Europe and a hub for transportation and the marketing systems, the numerous international commercial branch banks operated by Florentine and French families, and the sophisticated guild system of dyers and weavers in the southern Netherlands all played important roles in this trade. In the fifteenth century the latter region (formerly also called the Spanish Netherlands), contained roughly what is today Belgium; however, earlier in the Middle Ages it also encompassed the Franco-Belgian border areas of Artois and Picardy that once belonged to the powerful Dukes of Burgundy (Masschelein-Kleiner 1979: 29–30). The dyers', weavers', and painters' guilds (powerful craftsmen federations) often had elaborate legal regulations that assured high standards of production; for example, in guilds in the southern Netherlands workers were separated into distinct specialists as dyers of red and dyers of blue. Their use of natural vegetable dyes fixed to the fibers with mordants of metallic salts (such as alum or ferrous sulfate) to create colored yarns was carefully regulated to eliminate inferior quality (ibid. and Cavallo 1993: 25, 69). Guild restrictions established in Brussels in 1476 required master weavers to use **cartoons** supplied by painters (Cavallo 1993: 69); weavers were permitted "to modify the painter's cartoons in only limited specific ways, such as in details of color or vegetation or in the patterns of textiles that were represented" (Adelson 1994: 6).

Probably first used in northern Europe to embellish church interiors, tapestries provided visual aids for teaching religion to the illiterate, sub-divided long bare walls in the nave and choir, and offered warmth and insulation from cold stone walls. These expensive decorations were also used in royal and noble chambers in castle interiors. In some ways they may be considered the medieval equivalent of the modern cinema—tapestries appealed to audiences of every social level, as their visual message could be understood by all. Many people learned about historical events and themes of religious devotion through the panels hung in public spaces, where the story unfolded like a comic strip as a continuous narrative along a wall or around a room. While serving as educational instruction and political propanganda, tapestries also entertained. Tapestries functioned primarily as emblems of status and symbolized the wealth of their owners. As the possession of costly pictorial works was then a rarity, the display of splendid, enormously expensive tapestry sets covering rooms wall to wall indicated wealth and power that only the aristocracy could achieve. Moreover, like gold or silver plate, tapestries could be easily transported from castle to castle and hung quickly to convert an empty architectural space into a courtly environment and to establish immediately the status of the itinerant owner and his retinue. Tapestries were also displayed outdoors, hung on building facades as decoration for religious processions, court pageants, and parades, or carried on the battlefield to line the tents of rulers and nobles, and, by their conspicuous display, to remind visitors of the prominence of the occupant. They were considered valuable commodities and served to transfer wealth through inheritance or diplomatic, royal, aristocratic, or papal gifts. Francis I, king of France, owned two hundred tapestries according to inventories of the royal Garde-Meuble in 1542 and 1551; Henry VIII of England is recorded in the inventory at his death in 1547 as owning more than two thousand tapestries (Campbell 1995/96: 29; Joubert 1995: 81–84, 87). Referred to as "mobile frescoes of the north" by Delmarcel and others (Antwerp 1994), because like Italian frescoes they covered wall surfaces with images, the finest tapestries were, however, always more costly to produce than paintings; consequently, as items of great value, they were often recorded precisely in estate inventories. Tapestries were the most expensive and prestigious art form for centuries in northern Europe.

The world's largest and among the oldest and best documented of all surviving tapestry series, the *Apocalypse* series of eighty-four scenes, now in the Musée de la Tapisserie, Angers, was commissioned between 1377 and 1381 from Arras weavers by Louis I, Duke of Anjou, the French province to the west of the Loire valley with its

romantic late fifteenth-century *Lady with the Unicorn* series (Musée de Cluny, Paris) and the *Hunt of the Unicorn* series (Metropolitan Museum of Art, The Cloisters, New York), lack a similar degree of documentation as the *Apocalypse* series. Consequently, many disparate theories proposing identifications of both the Cluny and Cloisters Unicorn tapestry designers and weavers, and of the patron and iconography of the Cloisters's series, have been published (Cavallo 1993: 297–327; Joubert et. al. 1995: 52–56, cat. nos. 39–40).

FIG. 3 A weaver working at a high-warp, or vertical, loom. The finished tapestry fills the lower part of the warp. The bobbins, each of which carries the weft thread of a different color, hang from the edge of the woven cloth. The weaver works from the back of the tapestry. In order to see the front, he must either walk around to the front or peer through the warps to see a portion reflected in a mirror (Diderot 1771)

capital at Angers. Louis, brother of Charles V, King of France (r. 1364–80); of John, Duke of Berry; and of Philip the Bold, Duke of Burgundy, came from a family of lavish patrons. From the late fourteenth century on, the Angers series influenced subsequent tapestries. Their massive scale and sumptuous decorative quality established tapestries as essential works of art seen in the daily life of European courts. The best known of all tapestries, the

Until the late fifteenth century, the weaver was generally the designer responsible for transforming an iconographic narrative program into a visual image. Although the process is not fully understood, the design of fifteenth and many early sixteenth-century tapestries, especially those with complex allegorical programs, was often conceived by a learned scholar, rhetoretician, or ecclesiastic who created the narrative composition after receiving a commission from a patron. By the sixteenth century, an independent artist often painted a small finished model, called the ***petit patron,*** which the tapestry designer enlarged to a full-scale design, called the cartoon. The cartoon was usually painted on cloth in grisaille or with the colors indicated. Using either a high or low warp loom, several weavers worked on a single tapestry. They transformed the cartoon into a woven work of art, bringing to it color, shadow, and texture with special vegetable-dyed wools in a myriad of shades, using

where in the southern Netherlands and France where princes, nobles, the bourgeoisie, and church officials provided patronage, and the wool trade and cloth industry were most active. Fourteenth- to early sixteenth-century tapestries were traditionally attributed to specific French and south Netherlandish centers of production—from obscure beginnings around 1350 to 1400 in Paris, to a flowering in Arras fifty years later, to Tournai during the second half of the fifteenth century, until Tournai was superseded by Brussels about 1500. Thought of as suc-

FIG. 4 A low-warp workshop at the Gobelins Manufactory in Paris. On a low-warp loom the warp is stretched horizontally between two rollers, with the cartoon lying beneath the warps. Foot pedals manipulated the warp, thus freeing the weaver's hands and saving time. The great disadvantage of the low-warp loom was that the weaver, who works from the back of the tapestry, was unable to see the front until the entire tapestry was finished. (Diderot 1771)

dying and weaving techniques known since ancient Egypt. Working six days a week from morning to evening, a skilled weaver required a year to produce only one or two square meters of fine tapestry (Standen 1987: 4; Bennett 1992: 299).

Over the centuries, tapestry production flourished in various centers: in Brussels, Antwerp, Arras, Tournai, Lille, Ghent, Bruges, Paris, Beauvais, Aubusson, and else-

cessive centers in the history tapestry production, these are towns where itinerant artists and weavers were assumed to follow new sources of aristocratic patronage. As a tangible medium for capital investment by the Burgundian dukes and their Hapsburg successors, tapestry production was financed by wealthy patrons who moved their entourage to successive courts. The creation of new tapestry production centers was a political and

North Sea

ENGLAND

● Amsterdam

THE NETHERLANDS

London ●
Merton Abbey ●

● Bruges ● Antwerp

FLANDERS

BRABANT

Oudenaarde ● ● Brussels

ARTOIS ● ● Tournai

Lille ●
Arras

PICARDY

English Channel

● Beauvais

● Paris

● Orléans

● Angers ● Blois

BURGUNDY

LOIRE VALLEY

Atlantic Ocean

● Aubusson
● Felletin

CENTERS OF TAPESTRY PRODUCTION IN EUROPE

Mediterranean Sea

diplomatic tool of the aristocracy used to replace the cloth industry, then being lost to English rivals and to serve as a stimulus for new economic development in their own realms. Cavallo has questioned these traditional assumptions about the production of tapestries in successive historical centers and the ability to establish the style of a particular regional weaving center (Cavallo 1993: 57–61). On the basis of the industrial nature of weaving production, the portability of tapestries and cartoons, and the considerable variation in quality among tapestries thought to have been created in any one center, Cavallo argues for the use of the generic term "South Netherlands," rather than the more traditional specific attributions of Arras, Tournai, or Brussels for medieval tapestries. Only a few surviving medieval and Renaissance tapestries are now considered to be the productions of specific designers and workshops. Although there is documentation for the patrons and merchants who funded the industry, new archival research is needed.

By the late fifteenth and early sixteenth century, documentation of patronage and workshop activity in the court city Brussels and nearby Bruges, the international crossroads for commerce and art, enables one to postulate when, where, and for whom certain tapestries in this exhibition were designed and produced. Moreover, the late fifteenth-century introduction of weavers' marks on tapestry **borders** required by the Brussels painters' and weavers' guilds (Cavallo 1993: 69), scientific analyses of specific fibers, dyes, and stylistic motifs associated with weaving schools (Thurman 1979: 6), and heraldic research all help to determine the origin of a few tapestries of this period. These tools for research and comparisons with documented tapestries in other collections permit the identification and dating of many of the tapestries in Detroit and create a historical context for our collection.

The twenty tapestries in this exhibition illustrate a range of styles and designs. Scholarship reveals information about various intellectual conceptions, patrons and commissions, workshop production methods, weavers' models, and the technique of weaving itself. As the Detroit collection has not been published, much new information is given in this catalogue. While the specific content of some of the museum's early **millefleurs** tapestries remains enigmatic, the two earliest examples (CAT. NOS. 1–2) bear heraldic arms and inscriptions here identified for the first time as those of the Brachet, Tournemine, and other prominent families at the French courts of Louis XII and François I around 1500 to 1520. These two tapestries, like three other south Netherlandish fragments (CAT. NOS. 3–5), can also now be closely associated with tapestries in other collections to envision larger sets. The subjects of fifteenth- and sixteenth-century tapestries were often inspired by classical literature, period romances, plays, or prints. For the recently conserved *Triumph of Spring* (FIG. 1; CAT. NO. 10), the original design source, a 1537 woodcut by the Flemish Master A.P., is discussed with this allegorical Flemish tapestry of a Roman triumphal procession. Identified by specific stylistic motifs and color, it was woven in Bruges. The borders of this tapestry bear the date "1537" woven on one side and "1538" on the other, indicating that the weaving took a year or more to produce.

Another group of tapestries represents the achievements of the weaving workshops in Brussels from the early sixteenth century, the so-called golden age of the Brussels tapestry industry. Brussels was the capital of Brabant and the court city to Margaret of Austria, daughter of the Holy Roman Emperor Maximilian I. Through Margaret, the city and region received patronage from imperial Hapsburg and royal French courts in Vienna, Madrid, and Paris (cities, not coincidently, where the largest collections of European tapestries remain in museums today). Since Margaret cultivated new patronage of the arts, particularly tapestry weaving, Brussels took the lead in the first years of the sixteenth century as the Italian Renaissance pictorial style gradually took hold in northern European countries and as the Burgundian tapestry weaving centers at Arras and Tournai were in decline. The Brussels workshops flourished for more than two centuries because of superior designers, a modern guild organization, and a more efficient weaving technique using low-warp looms to accelerate production. The most important set of Brussels tapestries in the museum's collection is the group of *Virtues and Vices* (CAT. NOS. 6–9) woven in the first years of the sixteenth century. They consist of *Wrath* and *Pride*, two of the Seven Deadly Sins, and *Charity* and *Fortitude*, two of the Seven Virtues. As suggested by their nineteenth-century provenance, these may have been commissioned by the prominent Montmorency family of France.

Between 1516 and 1519, Brussels weaving ateliers completed the commission from Pope Leo X to weave the important series of the *Acts of the Apostles* after the ten cartoons of the lives of Saints Peter and Paul that the Italian Renaissance painter Raphael had created in Rome during 1515–16. Leo X intended for this series to hang on the walls of the Sistine Chapel under the frescoed ceiling painted by Michelangelo and below the earlier fifteenth-century frescos by Botticelli, Perugino, and others on the lateral walls. Raphael's High Renaissance design, using deep spatial perspective and a focus on the central figures in the narrative, made millefleurs and other late medieval tapestry styles appear outdated by the 1520s. Although the frontal plane is crowded with figures, the *Antique Battle Scene* (CAT. NO. 11), which Guy Delmarcel has identified as woven by the Brussels weaver François Tons, reflects the new Renaissance use of perspective and understanding of light effects gained from Raphael and also

subsequently called Gobelins. By the late sixteenth century the Gobelins' firm was so successful that the family became prominent at the French court and retired from their business. In turn, a small tapestry manufactory with Flemish weavers was opened on the former Gobelins' property in 1601 (Bennett 1992: 241). With the vast financial resources and commitment of Louis XIV in the 1660s, the Gobelins expanded to employ two-hundred and fifty weavers organized, not as a guild as in Brussels, but under the artistic director for the manufactory, the

FIG. 5 Detail from *Psyche Displaying Her Treasures to Her Sisters* (CAT. NO. 16)

from Flemish and Netherlandish artists who traveled and worked in Italy in the sixteenth century.

While Brussels continued to reign as the center for the production of tapestries from cartoons designed by Rubens and other Flemish and Italian artists through the seventeenth century, the French King Louis XIV and his Minister J.-B. Colbert established the **Gobelins Manufactory** in Paris in 1662. In their view, the age of individual private patronage of the arts had waned and only the king could rejuvenate the cultural life of the country. The royal manufactory owes its name to a family named Gobelin, who around 1450 opened a dyeing workshop on the edge of Paris on property that grew into a village

virtuoso painter and designer Charles LeBrun. Although it closed for five years in the 1690s, Gobelins became the most important tapestry factory of the late seventeenth and eighteenth centuries, producing a wide range of brilliantly colored weavings of a technical perfection never equaled. The Gobelins, whose works were sought throughout Europe, is well represented in this exhibition by two recently conserved tapestries depicting courtiers and peasants in leisurely pursuits: *February*, from the "Months of Lucas" series and *Winter* from the "Seasons of Lucas" series (CAT. NOS. 12–13).

As the Gobelins worked specifically for the Crown, other French manufactories were soon created by Louis

XIV and Colbert in order to encourage competition with Netherlandish workshops and to meet the extensive demand for tapestries from French aristocratic patrons. The **Beauvais Manufactory** was established in 1664 and a year later the weaving workshops in **Aubusson** received new royal privileges. Beauvais, the second royal French tapestry manufactory, founded in 1664 by Colbert, was subsidized and patronized by the Crown but operated as a private enterprise for over a century. Although weaving workshops had existed in the town of Aubusson since the Middle Ages, they received in 1665 the privilege of using the appellation "manufacture royale" for the tapestries they wove. *Jupiter and Callisto* (CAT. NO. 14) and two others from the same series of the Metamorphoses of Ovid (included in the exhibition) are dated about 1680; the coat-of-arms located in the upper border is that of Marguerite Colbert, and her husband, Vincent Hotman, seigneur of Fontenay. *Psyche Displaying Her Treasures*, designed by François Boucher (FIG. 5; CAT. NO. 16), another Beauvais tapestry, has been identified as belonging to the set of five commissioned in 1744 by the Spanish ambassador to France. Tapestry upholstery and furnishing panels were also produced by French manufactories in the eighteenth century, and the exhibition includes four Gobelins tapestry panels after Boucher designs (CAT. NO. 17), probably from firescreens, and a pair of armchairs, which are part of a set retaining its original Beauvais tapestry upholstery (CAT. NO. 18). For the changing interior decoration required for the eighteenth-century Parisian *salon* or the English country house, the Gobelins produced elegant "tapestry rooms" in which each wall surface was covered with tapestries and complemented with tapestry-upholstered furniture. Although the Gobelins and Beauvais factories closed in 1793 during the French Revolution, they reopened later as state-owned but diminished enterprises under Napoleon. In the nineteenth century the Gobelins primarily copied older tapestries and religious subjects after paintings by old masters while Beauvais specialized in furniture coverings. The prevailing concern of the Industrial Revolution for mass production, speed of execution, and profit derived from the use of new mechanized looms, the prohibitive expense of traditional tapestries, and their newly perceived status as *retardetaire*, rather than innovative, works of art (Bennett 1992: 299), led to a rapid decline in tapestry production and aesthetic merit during the nineteenth century.

To represent the revival of traditional high-quality weaving techniques in the late nineteenth and early twentieth centuries, the exhibition concludes with one of the most important Arts and Crafts tapestries now in America, the *Passing of Venus* (CAT. NO. 19), and the original gouache *petit patron* by Edward Burne-Jones, lent by the Metropolitan Museum of Art (FIG. 15). The tapestry, designed by Burne-Jones and J. Henry Dearle, and woven by William Morris and Company at **Merton Abbey**, in Surrey, England, was commissioned by local educator, patron, and businessman George G. Booth for the Detroit Institute of Arts's Woodward Avenue building, which opened in 1927. As first president of the Detroit Society of Arts and Crafts and president of *The Detroit News*, Booth and his wife Ellen Scripps Booth established the Cranbrook Educational Community and Academy of Art located north of Detroit in Bloomfield Hills, Michigan, and created the momentum for tapestry collecting and weaving in southeastern Michigan. In 1920 Booth, who had become a life-long disciple of William Morris and British design, acquired the Burne-Jones designed tapestry *David Instructing Solomon in the Building of the Temple*, woven at Merton Abbey in 1902–03, and lent by Christ Church, Cranbrook, to this exhibition. Booth's high standards of production required for the *Passing of Venus*, his acquisition of earlier tapestries, and his creation of an internationally recognized weaving department to teach design and modern techniques at Cranbrook were catalysts that led to the creation of the textile collection at the Detroit Institute of Arts.

The arrival in Detroit of European-trained painting, sculpture, and textile specialist William Valentiner in 1921 (who served from 1908–14 as the first curator of decorative arts, tapestries, and the Morgan collection at the Metropolitan Museum of Art; from 1921–24 as the Detroit Institute of Arts' expert and advisor, and as museum director from 1924–45) and of Adele Weibel as curator of textiles in 1927 enabled the museum to develop a significant textile collection over the next five decades (Sterne 1980: 92–96, 157, 177, 396–97; Peck 1991: 64–65, 79). Sixty-six of the seventy-five tapestries presented in this catalogue and checklist entered the museum's collections before Weibel's departure in the 1960s. This exhibition of our European tapestry collection is intended to renew appreciation and study of this significant part of the museum's collection. It is hoped that continued encouragement from the public will lead to further conservation, exhibitions, and publications on our European tapestries. With the enlightened spirit of support established in Michigan, the "woven splendor" of European tapestry will continue, as William Morris advocated, to inspire artists today and to be celebrated as a worthy artistic endeavor.

THE NOBLEST
OF THE WEAVING
ARTS IS TAPESTRY . . .
SPECIAL EXCELLENCIES CAN BE EXPECTED
FROM IT. DEPTH OF TONE, RICHNESS OF
COLOUR, AND EXQUISITE GRADATION OF TINTS
ARE EASILY TO BE OBTAINED IN TAPESTRY;
AND IT ALSO DEMANDS THAT CRISPNESS AND
ABUNDANCE OF BEAUTIFUL DETAIL WHICH
WAS THE ESPECIAL CHARACTERISTIC OF
ॐ FULLY DEVELOPED MEDIEVAL ART. ॐ

William Morris (1834-96), from his lecture
on 'Textiles' (London 1888:15)

Catalogue of the Exhibition

[1] *Millefleurs Tapestry with the Arms of the Brachet and other Families of Orléans, Blois, and Anjou*

ca. 1500–20; Probably designed in France (Loire),
woven in the southern Netherlands
Wool and silk; 9 ft. 6 in. × 10 ft. 1 in. (2.9 m × 3 m)
Founders Society Purchase, General Membership Fund (56.190)

INSCRIPTIONS
Initials M and I tied together at corners. Mottos on scrolls in border: VAILLE QVE VAILLE LORS SE VERRAS ("One goes as one goes, then one shall see"). Heraldic Identifications: Arms at center: Gaillard of Orléans and Blois (upper left); Compaing of Orléans (upper right); Maidon of Orléans (lower left); Lesbahy of Blois (lower right); Brachet of Orléans (center). Arms in border at top: Brachet of Orléans. Arms in border at bottom: Cherbaye of Blois. Arms in borders at sides: Unidentified (left); Jarry of Anjou (right).

PROVENANCE
Probably made for a member of the Brachet family of Orléans, ca. 1500–20; Count of Charencay, France (probably with pendant now in the Burrell Collection, Glasgow, Scotland); Caroline Bernheimer, Munich; Adolph Loewi, Los Angeles.

EXHIBITIONS
Tournai 1970: no. 7; Detroit 1984: not in catalogue.

REFERENCES
Weibel 1957: 89–90; *Art Quarterly* 1957: 226–27; Asselberghs 1974: 23.

RELATED WORKS
A tapestry with variant arms and a wild man rather than a griffin and of similar dimensions and composition (FIG. 6) is now in the Burrell Collection, Glasgow, Scotland (Wells 1959: 15, 14 illus.).

This piece, with its complicated heraldic program, attests to the importance of tapestry in conveying the status of the commissioning family and in asserting the important alliances, both familial and social, to which they lay claim. A **millefleurs** design serves as the elaborate backdrop for the enigmatic display of a heraldic shield. Suspended from a barren tree, enclosed within a walled garden, guarded by a winged griffin, the shield with five distinct sets of arms makes pointed reference to an intricate network of relations among noble families in the Loire valley.

A tapestry from the Burrell Collection in Glasgow, Scotland (FIG. 6), is closely linked to the Detroit piece. A coat of arms at its center also hangs from a lifeless tree, isolated within an enclosed space. A wooden fence replaces the crenelated stone wall and, in place of the griffin, a wild man stands guard. Both share a richly designed **border** embellished with mottos. Family arms anchor the four cardinal points, and a pair of entwined initials adorn each of the four corners. The two pieces perhaps were once joined to form a whole or part of a whole tapestry.

Recent heraldic research by Philippe Palasi (DIA curatorial files) has identified the arms and ciphers. Common to both tapestries is the conspicuous reference to the Brachet family, whose most prominent member Jean (d. after 1541) served as tax-collector for the region of Orléans and secretary to the Duke of Orléans, the future King Louis XII (r. 1498–1515). The Brachet arms, signaled by a seated pointer, appear at the top of both tapestries and in the center of each of the heraldic shields. The knotted rope that separates the border from the central field refers to the Brachet family as well; the motif appears on the exterior of the family's late medieval mansion in Orléans.

The arms of no fewer than thirteen different families from the circle of Louis XII appear on the two tapestries. Those on the Detroit piece all refer to members of the immediate family of Jean Brachet. The Glasgow tapestry features arms of both family members and unrelated friends from the French world of finance, including those of the illustrious Cottereau family. Pierre Cottereau served as treasurer of France and Secretary to the King.

[1] *Millefleurs Tapestry with the Arms of the Brachet and other Families of Orléans, Blois, and Anjou*

The monograms M and I [J] found in the corners suggest that the occasion for the commission of these tapestries seems likely to have been the celebration of a matrimonial alliance with prominent families in the circle of Louis XII. The letters M and I (long erroneously identified; London 1938; Weibel 1957; Wells 1959; Asselberghs 1974) perhaps refer to Marie Brachet, granddaughter of Jean Brachet, and to Jean Compaing, whose arms are among those in the central shield of the Detroit piece. Marie Brachet and Jean Compaing were married in 1506, a date that coincides credibly with both the style and technique of the tapestry. Alternatively, they might refer to participants in an unrecorded marriage between a Brachet family member and a member of the Cherbaye-Villebresme family, whose arms appear on the bottom of the Glasgow tapestry. The interrelated and complex heraldic designs suggest that the Brachet patron had a French designer and heraldist devise the **cartoons** for a set of tapestries, which in turn were likely sent to the southern Netherlands for weaving.   🙚 APD/MH

FIG. 6 *Millefleurs Tapestry with Coat of Arms Guarded by a Wild Man,* southern Netherlands, ca. 1500–20. Wool and silk, 9 ft. 10 ¾ in. × 10 ft. ¼ in. Glasgow Museums: The Burrell Collection.

[2] *Shepherd and Shepherdess*

ca. 1500–30; probably designed in France,
woven in the southern Netherlands
Wool and silk; 6 ft. 11 in. × 13 ft. 11 in. (2.1 × 4.2 m)
Bequest of Eleanor Clay Ford (77.9)

INSCRIPTIONS

Above the shepherdess: MOUT ME PLAIST CE GETIL
BOUCHAGE/IE LAYME TANT QUE IE NEN HOBBE/ET
BREF POUR FAIR BON MESNAGE/IE NE VEUIL QUE MA
GARDEROBE (*I do like this pretty grove! I like it so much that I
shan't leave it; and, in a word, in order to live here happily all I
need is my wardrobe*).   To the right of the shepherd:
BERGERETTE PLAISANT ET SAIGE/METRYEZ VOUS
POINT SOUS VOSTRE ROBE/CE QUE VOUS BAILLERAI EN
GAIGE/AFIN QUE ON NE LE VOUS DESROBE (*Pretty, wise
little shepherdess, won't you put under your dress what I will give
you as my token of love so that no one can steal it from you?*)

PROVENANCE

Probably made for a member of the Tournemine family, possibly Françoise de Tournemine, ca. 1515–30; Charles Mège, Paris,
by 1889; Parish-Watson and Company, New York, Sale Sept. 26,
1928; Eleanor Clay Ford, Grosse Pointe Shores, Michigan.

EXHIBITIONS

Detroit 1928: no. 103; Detroit 1984: not in catalogue.

REFERENCES

Migeon 1909: 17, 2 illus.; Cavallo 1979: 30–39; Cavallo 1993: 485–
87, fig. 154.

RELATED WORKS

A closely related tapestry, *Shepherd and Shepherdess Making
Music* (FIG. 7), is in the Metropolitan Museum of Art, New York
(Cavallo 1993: no. 35). A third tapestry *Shepherd and Shepherdess*
(FIG. 8) is in the collection of the Mobilier National, Paris
(Cavallo 1993: fig. 155). A small fragment of another companion
piece of the Detroit tapestry is in the collection of the Manufac-
ture Nationale des Gobelins, Paris (Paris 1928: no. 56).

In this **millefleurs** tapestry a shepherd and shepherdess tending their flock stand and converse on either
side of a fruit tree within an orchard, in a composition
that recalls the iconography of Adam and Eve. Near each
figure is a verse of four lines in Old French. At the base of
the tree is a seated dog (often a symbol of fidelity) and to
the right of the shepherd is a ram. An armorial shield,
quartered gold and azure, hangs by a red buckled strap
from the branches of the central tree.

Noting similarities in the subject matter, composition, and tone of the inscribed verses, and in the design
and color of the background, Cavallo has linked the
Detroit tapestry with two other millefleur tapestries depicting bucolic themes (Cavallo 1993: 485–486). The New
York version shows the two rustic protagonists engaged

in music-making (FIG. 7), while one in Paris shows a
shepherd walking toward a seated shepherdess (FIG. 8).
The inclusion of the same motifs in all three tapestries
gives further indication that they probably derived from
a single series of **cartoons** or were conceived as part of a
set. A grazing sheep appears, though sometimes reversed,
in each of the three tapestries, and the New York and
Paris tapestries share a second sheep depicted in a fore-
shortened frontal view. Whether the three were part of a
larger set has been to date impossible to determine (Cavallo
1993: 487). The New York tapestry, some ten inches taller
than the Detroit or Paris pieces, has sustained minor losses
at its upper edge and gives a sense of the original height of
the three pieces. The Detroit tapestry is the only one that
survives with its full width (Cavallo 1979: 31–32).

FIG. 7 *Shepherd and Shepherdess Making Music*, southern
Netherlands, ca. 1500. Wool and silk, 7 ft. 8½ in. × 9 ft. 7 in.
The Metropolitan Museum of Art, Bequest of Susan Vanderpoel
Clark, 1967. (67.155.8)

All three tapestries rely on verses, filled with pun-
ning rhymes and rich with double entendres, to convey
their meaning. Playing off variations of the word *"robe"*
("dress"), the verses in the Detroit tapestry describe an
artful duel between the shepherdess who thinks of noth-
ing but fashion and the shepherd eager to discover the
woman beneath the clothes. Richard Katz has connected
the style of the language, particularly that on the Paris
tapestry, to the poetry at the Burgundian court written by
a group of writers known as the *grands rhétoriqueurs*
(Cavallo 1993: 484). The text of the verses likely derives
from popular songs, such as the *pastourelle*, a medieval
lyric that typically recounts a shepherd's persistent

FIG. 8 *Shepherd and Shepherdess,* southern Netherlands, ca. 1500. Wool and silk, 6 ft. 10 in. × 10 ft. 4 in. Collection Mobilier National, Paris.

attempts at seducing a reluctant shepherdess (Paden 1995: 713–714). Such poems appealed as they could be read on several levels—as a bawdy joke, an allegory, a moral tale, or social satire. Cavallo characterized the Detroit, Paris, and New York tapestries as a "satirical allegory in which women are victims of virtues. . . or vices. . ., and men are bound to the passions of flesh, all this expressed in terms of the simple, natural rustic or shepherd" (1993: 487).

The same shield that appears at the center of the Detroit *Shepherd and Shepherdess* features prominently in both the Paris and New York tapestries. Part of the original woven fabric in the Detroit and Paris pieces, the arms are a later insert in the New York tapestry (Cavallo 1993: 483). The restored arms may have duplicated the original shield, perhaps removed, as was common during the French Revolution, or although improbable, they may be a later copy after the Detroit and Paris arms.

Philippe Palasi has proposed that the previously unidentified arms in the three tapestries are those of the French noble family of Tournemine in Brittany, who were active at the court of François I (reigned 1515–1547) (DIA curatorial files). The family's most celebrated member was Françoise, known at court as the "Amirale d'Annebaud" after her third husband, Claude d'Annebaud, admiral and marshal of France (Lapeyre and Scheurer 1978: 117). The courtly flavor of the verses and the tapestries' stylistic compatibility with Françoise's dates make it tempting to link them with her patronage.   ॐ APD/MH

[2] *Shepherd and Shepherdess*

[3] *Millefleurs Fragment: Neptune, God of the Waters*

FIG. 9 *Hercules and the Nemean Lion*, southern Netherlands, ca. 1500–25. Wool and silk, 9 ft. 1 in. × 10 ft. 10 in. Musée des Arts Décoratifs, Paris.

[3] *Millefleurs Fragment: Neptune, God of the Waters*

ca. 1500–25; designed in France, woven in northern France or the southern Netherlands
Wool and silk; 8 ft. 1 in. × 3 ft. 3¾ in. (2.4 × 1 m)
Gift of Mr. and Mrs. Douglas F. Roby (58.414)

INSCRIPTION
On the tunic: NEPTVNVS RE[X]

PROVENANCE
Said to come from the collection of the Princes of Ligne, Belgium; French and Co., New York; acquired as the gift of Mr. and Mrs. Douglas F. Roby, Grosse Pointe, Michigan.

EXHIBITIONS
Brussels 1947: 9; Bruges 1960: no. 137; Detroit 1960: no. 154.

REFERENCES
Weibel 1959: 96–97; Asselberghs 1974: 23.

RELATED VERSIONS
See CAT. NO. 4. *Hercules and the Nemean Lion* (FIG. 9), is in the Musée des Arts Décoratifs, Paris, formerly in the the collection of Jules Maciet (Göbel 1928, II: pl. 317; Demotte 1924: pl. 127).

[4] *Millefleurs Fragment: Jupiter, King of the Gods*

[4] *Millefleurs Fragment: Jupiter, King of the Gods*

ca. 1500–25; designed in France, woven in northern France or the southern Netherlands
Wool and silk; 8 ft. 1 in. × 3 ft. 3 ¾ in. (246 × 93 cm)
Gift of Mrs. Edsel B. Ford and K.T. Keller (58.415)

INSCRIPTION
On the border of the cloak: IVPITER (followed by letters which cannot be interpreted with certainty)

PROVENANCE
Said to have come from the collection of the Princes of Ligne, Belgium; French and Co., New York; acquired as the gift of Eleanor Clay Ford, Grosse Pointe Shores, Michigan, and Mr. and Mrs. K.T. Keller, Grosse Pointe, Michigan.

EXHIBITIONS
Brussels 1947: 9; Bruges 1960: no. 137; Detroit 1960: no. 155.

REFERENCES
Ackerman 1932: 11, pl. 29; Weibel 1959: 96–97; Asselberghs 1974: 23.

RELATED WORKS
See CAT. NO. 3. *Hercules and the Nemean Lion* (see FIG. 9), is in the Musée des Arts Décoratifs, Paris, formerly in the collection of Jules Maciet (Göbel 1928, II: pl. 317; Demotte 1924: pl. 127).

Classical mythology merges with a French court aesthetic in these two refined **millefleurs** tapestry fragments, which show Jupiter and Neptune dressed in the elegant style of French nobles around 1500. Neptune, wearing a jeweled soft bi-cornered hat with a turned-up brim (inspired by Near Eastern fashions), high boots with a prominent cuff, and wide-toed shoes with an exaggerated point, carries his identifying attributes: two fish and a large trident. Jupiter wears a jeweled crown and carries a scepter. His attribute, the eagle, stands at his feet.

These fragments may have served as pendant images framing a central narrative scene or, more likely, they each were the central figures in a pair of tapestries taken from a set depicting the gods of Olympus. The Musée des Arts Décoratifs in Paris owns a related tapestry that depicts the demi-god Hercules (FIG. 9). Similarities in the graceful pose, elegant courtly dress, and facial features among the three figures suggest a common designer or workshop. Because the Hercules tapestry has not been cut down as drastically as the Detroit pieces, it provides a better sense of their original size and composition. All three could be said to belong to a French tradition of "heroic" tapestries, such as those devoted to the Male and Female Worthies. These were ambitious cycles that depicted large-scale figures drawn from literature or mythology, isolated within an abstracted, nonspecific setting.

The overall design and subject of these tapestries suggests a French source, but the widespread appeal of a French aesthetic at this time prevents suggesting an exact place of their manufacture. The tapestries' alleged provenance in the collections of the Princes of Ligne, who owned a castle near Tournai where the tapestries most likely hung, suggests that the tapestries might have been created in that weaving center. In any event, the style of the tapestry evokes the retardetaire late medieval aesthetic of naturalism and rich color associated with the refined taste of Louis XII, king of France in the early years of the sixteenth century.   ❧ APD/MH

[5] *Eros Triumphant*

[5] *Eros Triumphant*

ca. 1500–20; designed in northern France; woven in
the southern Netherlands
Wool and silk; 9 ft. 6 in. × 3 ft. 6 in. (2.9 × 1 m)
Founders Society Purchase, Ralph Harman Booth
Bequest Fund (35.6)

INSCRIPTIONS
Above the head of Eros, fragments of verse: JE FRAPE TOUT A
TORT ET A.../DE ARS ET DE DARS LES CHASTES.../MAIS A
LA FIN QUELQUE IOUSSE [?]/LA MORT SURVIENT QUI
TOUT M...(With my art and my arrows I strike the chaste...but
finally [?]...it is death that comes and... all...)

PROVENANCE
Marczell von Nemes Sale, Part II, Munich, June 16–19, 1931, no.
296, ill.; A. S. Drey, New York (as Touraine).

EXHIBITIONS
Hartford 1951: no. 84; Cleveland 1966: no. VII-25; Paris 1973: no.
60; New York 1974: no. 65; Detroit 1978: no. 20; Detroit 1982: 1, 7.

REFERENCES
Weibel 1935a: 76–81; Shepherd 1961: 172–173; Wixom 1961: 183;
Sterling 1966: 23–26, pl. 20; Asselberghs 1974: 23.

RELATED WORKS
A set of three millefleurs tapestries that share the theme of
Petrarchan triumphs, *Triumph of Youth; Triumph of Eternity*,
and *Triumph of Time*, in the Cleveland Museum of Art, have
been traditionally associated with the Detroit tapestry. An early
sixteenth century manuscript (MS 5066, Bibliothèque de
l'Arsenal, Paris) of a French translation of Petrarch's *Trionfi*
provides a source for the image and iconography of the tapestry
(Shepherd 1961: 158–63, figs. 1–3).

This early sixteenth-century tapestry fragment depicts Eros, the god of Love, who was most likely the
central figure of a larger tapestry within a series. The
classically inspired theme refers to the power of love and
to the greater power of death.

Eros is represented as a winged muscular young
man, blindfolded and wearing a chain-mail skirt. Contemporary sources identify him more precisely as Cupido
or Cupidon to distinguish him from Cupid who is represented as a child. In the modeling of the figure, Weibel
(1935: 75) detects the influence of Italian Renaissance
painters such as Mantegna; Wixom (1966: 183), links it to
thirteenth-century medieval manuscripts. Noting both
Italian and French qualities, Sterling (1961: 24) places the
figure style in the milieu of fifteenth-century Provençal
painting, specifically in the circle of the Master of the
Retable of Boulbon, a painter influenced by Piero della
Francesca.

The representation of Eros as victor and the implied
reference to a battle involving "the chaste" and "death" in
the inscription relate the theme of the tapestry to the
fourteenth-century *Trionfi* of Petrarch. Petrarch's work
describes a succession of battles between allegorical figures:
Love conquers Power, Chastity subdues Love, Death van-
quishes Chastity, Fame prevails over Death, and Time
eclipses Fame. The battles conclude with the triumph of
Eternity, the most powerful figure of all, over Time.

In a telescopic presentation of the first two rounds of
Petrarch's series, the Detroit fragment depicts both Love
vanquishing Power and Love's defeat, in turn, by Chastity.
The armored figures, once mighty princes and warriors
(their faces are modern restorations), lie trampled at the
feet of Eros; the sword tip entering from the right side is the
weapon of the now-missing figure of Chastity, who dis-
arms Eros by cutting his bowstring.

While Petrarch's *Trionfi* was widely illustrated in
fifteenth-century Italian paintings and manuscripts, the
source for the tapestry's unusual iconography was either
directly or indirectly a contemporary French translation of
Petrarch (Shepherd 1961: 172–73). In a departure from
Italian illustrations that show the defeated allegories crushed
beneath the wheels of a triumphal chariot, the French
manuscript (MS. 5066, Bibliothèque de l'Arsenal, Paris),
like the Detroit tapestry, shows an isolated figure labeled as
"Cupido" standing directly on top of his armored adversar-
ies, who are listed in the manuscript as Jupiter, Neptune,
and Plato. The debt to a French manuscript for its iconography and composition suggests that *Eros Triumphant* was
probably designed by a French designer in the early sixteenth century.

The Detroit tapestry has been repeatedly associated
with a group of tapestries in the Cleveland Museum of Art
which also allude to the theme of Petrarch's *Trionfi* (Weibel
1935a; Shepherd 1961: 172; Cleveland 1966: 336–341; Paris
1973: 147–155). The Cleveland works are believed to have
been ordered by Charles d'Amboise (d. 1511), a powerful
noble in the court of Louis XII (reigned 1498–1515), for the
redecoration of his Loire valley chateau between 1498 and
1511. In unpublished research Adolfo Cavallo disputes that
association, concluding that the Detroit piece not only
belongs to a different iconographic tradition from the
Cleveland pieces but also shares little with them in its
figural style (1978, DIA curatorial files). While Cavallo's
findings do not preclude the possibility that the piece once
belonged to Charles d'Amboise, they do beg for more
documentation in establishing a clear link between the
Detroit and Cleveland tapestries. ❧ APD/MH

THE VIRTUES AND VICES TAPESTRIES

The subject of Virtues and Vices enjoyed great success in late medieval sermons, devotional literature, and moralizing treatises. While they could vary in composition and number, they were commonly conceived in sets of seven. One canon of Virtues was made up of four cardinal virtues—Prudence, Temperance, Fortitude, and Justice—and three theological virtues—Faith, Hope, and Charity. The Vices were often represented as the Seven Deadly Sins—Pride, Envy, Wrath, Sloth, Avarice, Gluttony, and Lust.

Tapestry designers in sixteenth-century Brussels particularly favored themes that pitted allegorical figures against each other in a moral contest. Numerous Brussels tapestries showed variations of the Psychomachia, which presented the Virtues and Vices in armored combat. Tapestry series depicted elaborate histories of Christian Redemption, in which the Virtues and Vices contend for the fate of all humanity. Another form of allegorical contest shows a sinful man in the courtroom of God, prosecuted by Justice and Truth, but defended by Mercy and Peace. This set of four tapestries from Brussels presents in each the personification of a single Virtue or Vice, who is enthroned within an elegant canopy in the center and surrounded by a courtly retinue of figures drawn from literary, historical and biblical sources.

These complex allegorical tapestries are among the earliest of the so-called altar or stage-set tapestries, which are characterized by the use of thin jeweled columns and other architectural devices to organize the scene. These form a series of small compartments, each closed at the back with a curtain, which recall the open-front pavilions that served as the setting for morality plays and ceremonial pageants in the later Middle Ages. The compartments permit the simultaneous presentation of several episodes, all of which relate in an intricate and recondite way to the central theme. A similar technique was employed in fifteenth-century polyptychs as well as in prints. Woodbook versions of the *Biblia Pauperum*, for example, employ architectural bays, spandrels, and arches to organize the composition and to establish typological links between the Old and New Testaments. The stage-set device proved a favorite organizational motif for tapestries in the fifteenth and early sixteenth centuries.

Other late fifteenth- and early sixteenth-century examples that employ the stage-set composition include *History of the Virgin* (Patrimonio Nacional, Madrid); the *Scene from the Life of a Young King* (Musée du Louvre, Paris, Inv. OA 10932, see Amaury Lefébure in Paris 1985:

50–51); the *Christ the Judge on the Throne of Majesty and other Subjects* (Metropolitan Museum of Art, New York, inv. nos. 53.80, 53.81, 41.100.214); and *Wisdom and Justice* (State Hermitage Museum, St. Petersburg). The **borders** of the Detroit tapestries were added later; similar borders exist on a *David and Bathsheba* tapestry in the Nationalmuseum, Stockholm, and on a tapestry in the J.B. Speed Museum, Louisville, Kentucky (Guy Delmarcel, DIA curatorial files).

As Delmarcel and Souchal have shown for another early sixteenth-century Brussels tapestry series representing the *Triumphs of the Seven Virtues,* what at first appears to be an incoherent design composition of individual figures randomly grouped in scenes around a central personified virtue can be better understood through identifying the intellectual relationships among the figures based on what may now be obscure literary sources, classical mythology, or medieval treatises (Souchal 1979: 103–53; Delmarcel 1979: 155–169).

Precise identifications of the figures in the Hearst tapestries and a convincing explanation of their relationship to one another have remained elusive, although Weibel and Robinson have attempted to decipher the various scenes (1955). They are likely drawn from contemporary theater, especially morality and mystery plays. The presentation of the personifications and related figures in the Detroit tapestries evokes a medieval mise-en-scène, and the use of identifying inscriptions found on two of the tapestries (*Fortitude* and *Pride*) may also relate to late medieval theatrical practices, which employed placards to identify characters (Cavallo 1993: 34). In the sixteenth century, the Brussels Chambre de Rhetorique organized lavish theatrical productions, pageants, and parades to celebrate religious holidays or to honor the arrival of sovereigns and princes to the city (Brussels 1976: 101). Tapestries often adorned the processional route and in some cases were designed specifically for that purpose (Cavallo 1993: 29). In a further demonstration of the fluidity between tapestry and drama, documents show that some of the same people who designed the dramas and tableaux vivants that were part of these urban spectacles also designed tapestries (Cavallo 1993: 34–36).

This group of four tapestries almost certainly formed part of a larger set though it is impossible to know how many tapestries would have completed it. Given their large size, it is difficult to imagine a setting, even the nave of a large church, that could accommodate an ensemble of Seven Virtues and Seven Vices. The figures' costumes, jewelry, and hair styles appear to be

[6] Detail of *Fortitude*

contemporary rather than historical, thus dating them to the first decade of the sixteenth century. Their monumental scale, high-quality weaving, and distinguished provenance suggest that they were a noble commission, perhaps for a member of the Montmorency-Luxembourg family—for centuries prominent among the high officers of the French crown—whose descendants sold them in the nineteenth century.   ᴈ APD/MH

[6] *Fortitude*

ca. 1500–1510; Southern Netherlands (probably Brussels)
Wool and silk; 12 ft. 8 in. × 21 ft. 8 in. (3.7 × 6.6 m)
Gift of the William Randolph Hearst Foundation (55.521)

PROVENANCE
Antoinette de Montmorency-Luxembourg; Baron Felix d'Hunol-
stein; Duveen Brothers, New York; William Randolph Hearst.

EXHIBITIONS
Paris 1880: no. 5

REFERENCES
Müntz 1902: pls. VII and VIII; Ackerman 1940: 187–210; Weibel
and Robinson 1955; Weibel and Robinson 1956: 60–63; Detroit
1971: 124; Asselberghs 1974: 23; Brussels 1976: 100.

RELATED WORKS
CAT. NOS. 7–9. A duplicate of the left section of this tapestry is in
the Archeological Museum, Madrid (Sanchez Beltrán 1983: 49–
50). Another fragment duplicating the central section was sold
at Hôtel Drouot, Paris, November 14, 1975, lot 156.14

DESCRIPTION AND INSCRIPTIONS

In the center, a figure labeled FORTITVDO (Fortitude), armed with a long spear, sits on a throne, with her
feet on her attribute of a lion. Around her appear an array
of figures including a woman on the left holding a castle-
shaped fountain and on the right a figure perhaps
representing Faith holding an orb and cross. Below on the
left stands Boldness, who wears a helmet and whose
garment bears the inscription FIDENTIA, and the kneeling figure of Gluttony, identified by the inscription GVLA
on the enframement beneath her. On the right is a group
of male Worthies: a king, with crown and sceptre; Hercules, labeled HERCVLIS on his garment, wearing armor;
and Charlemagne, with the inscription KAROLVS, beneath him.

In the lower left section appears the enthroned
figure of Avarice, labeled AVARITIA on her hem. Before
her kneels the figure of Good Counsel (a worn inscription
on his sleeve likely said CONSILIVM) and the Old Testament king Ahab, labeled ACHAB on the lower edge of his
cloak, offering a casket of coins.

In the upper section at the extreme left, a boy is
presented to an old man by two women, above them the
names I[N]TELLECT[US] (Understanding) and COG-
NITIO (Knowledge). In the compartment second from
the left sits Gluttony (GVLA inscribed above her head),
cutting a cake upon her lap. Two women approach with
food and drink. One may be identified as Buffoonery by
a faded inscription ([SCVRRIL?]ITAS) above her head.

[6] *Fortitude*

In the lower right section, a female figure sits on soft
pillows. She may be Sloth, as suggested by the figure riding
on an ass in the heart-shaped compartment above her
head; or she may be Justice, who requires repose to
consider her judgment and whose soft pillows signify the
mercy that tempers it. Below are Desire (DESIDERA-
TIO), Cowardice (PVSILLANINITAS in the border), and
Courage (FORTITVDO).

The background of the compartment second from the left shows a meeting of Esau (ESAV) and Jacob (IACOB). In the foreground, Judith (labeled JUDITH on her garment) kneels before Holofernes (OLOFERNES appears above his head). In the right corner, the Holy Spirit (labeled SP[IRITU]S S[AN]CT[U]S) crowns Piety (PIETAS) and Fear of God (TIMOR), both identified by inscriptions on their garments. ❧ APD/MH

[7] *Charity*

ca. 1500–1510; Southern Netherlands (probably Brussels)
Wool and silk; 12 ft. 8 in. × 20 ft. 10 in. (3.7 × 6.4 m)
Gift of the William Randolph Hearst Foundation (55.520)

PROVENANCE

Antoinette de Montmorency-Luxembourg; Baron Felix d'Hunolstein; Duveen Brothers, New York; William Randolph Hearst.

EXHIBITIONS

Paris 1880: no. 7

REFERENCES

Müntz 1902: pls. VII and VIII; Ackerman 1940: 187–210; Weibel and Robinson 1955; Weibel and Robinson 1956: 60–63; Detroit 1971: 124; Asselberghs 1974: 23; Brussels 1976: 100.

RELATED WORKS

CAT. NOS. 6, 8–9. A duplicate fragment of the right bottom section of the tapestry was sold at Parke-Bernet, New York, December 3–4, 1944, lot 107.

DESCRIPTION

No inscriptions occur on this tapestry to substantiate various interpretations. Christ enthroned may personify the virtue of Charity. Seated to the left are Faith, identified by her book, and Mercy, with her lily. On the right are Humility, suggested by her folded hands, and Justice, who carries an unsheathed sword. At his feet a figure who may represent the notion of Long Duration holds up a ring, a symbol of eternity. The mirror held by the woman below Christ at the left suggests that she may be Prudence, Luxuria (Riotous Living), or Vanity, all of whom are associated with mirrors. None of the other figures can be identified.

In the lower left section, a young woman and a young man kneel before an enthroned figure, whose book suggests that she might be Faith; the other two Theological Virtues, Hope and Charity, may be the figures who flank her.

In the two compartments in the upper left corner, a kneeling woman is presented to an enthroned Christ, who is flanked by Hope, identified by her attribute of an anchor, and an unidentified figure. The woman's sponsor is Mercy who carries her attribute of a lily. In the lower right section, a woman kneels before a king; perhaps she is the Queen of Sheba before King Solomon or Queen Esther presented by Mordecai to King Ahasuerus. In the two sections in the upper right, the Ark of the Covenant is carried in triumphant procession by high priests.

[7] *Charity*

[8] *Pride*

ca.1500–1510; Southern Netherlands (probably Brussels)
Wool and silk; 12 ft. 4 in. × 22 ft. (3.8 × 6.7 m)
Gift of the William Randolph Hearst Foundation (55.519)

PROVENANCE

Antoinette de Montmorency-Luxembourg; Baron Felix d'Hunol-
stein; Duveen Brothers, New York; William Randolph Hearst.

EXHIBITIONS

Paris 1880: no. 4

REFERENCES

Müntz 1902: pls. VII and VIII; Ackerman 1940: 187–210; Weibel
and Robinson 1955; Weibel and Robinson 1956: 60–63; Detroit
1971: 124; Asselberghs 1974: 23.

RELATED WORKS

CAT. NOS. 6–7, 9.

DESCRIPTION AND INSCRIPTIONS

In the center is the figure of Pride, labeled SVPERBIA,
who holds a long sceptre and gazes into a mirror held by
an unidentifed figure. Pride is sitting under a canopy
bearing an inscription from the Lord's Prayer. A modern
repair renders this difficult to read: ET NA [...]I[N]DVCAS
N[O]S [IN TENTATIONEM] SED LIB[ER]A NOS A
MA[LO] ("and lead us not into temptation but deliver us
from evil"). A small escutcheon on the canopy also refers
to Pride, who is represented riding upon her attribute of
a camel. Though inscriptions appear next to several
other figures, most are too faint to decipher. At the left, an
illegible inscription appears directly below a woman ges-
turing in surprise. Vanity (identified by VANTIA on her
dress) stands near her, pointing upward toward Pride. In
the center, sits Hypocrisy, labeled UPOCRISIS, who fin-
gers her rosary. At the right is seated a woman who places
a string of beads around the neck of a kneeling girl,
identified by an illegible inscription beneath the train of
her dress.

In the lower left, the princely figure of Fear of God,
labeled TIMOR on his hat, presides as judge over a court.
Men of Greater, Lesser, and Average moral quality, inscribed MAIOR, MINOR, and EQUALIS, respectively,
present their case before three women, of whom Humility (HVMILITAS) alone is named. One of the women
may be Peace, whose symbolic dove is perched on the
hand of Humility.

In the upper section at the extreme left, the principal figures are identified as Daniel (DANIEL on his
garment) kneeling before Nebuchadnezzar (NABVMO -
MONOSO), King of Babylon. Second from the left,
Abraham, marked by his name (ABRAHA[M]), kneels
before three angels.

[8] *Pride*

In the lower right corner, the enthroned figure in
the center may be identified by the attribute of the open
book as Wisdom or Faith. To the left stands Temperance
holding her attribute of a clock. Other figures approach,
bearing gifts. A woman, perhaps Wrath, identified by an
illegible inscription, gesticulates wildly.

In the upper section, at the extreme right are two seated figures: Piety (PIETAS written above her head) with the lamb, on the left, and Faith with a book, on the right. The allusion to LVXURIA, named on the enframement, is not clear.

[9] *Wrath*

ca.1500–1510; Southern Netherlands (probably Brussels)
Wool and silk; 12 ft. 6 in. × 22 ft. (3.8 × 6.7 m)
Gift of the William Randolph Hearst Foundation (55.522)

PROVENANCE
Antoinette de Montmorency-Luxembourg; Baron Felix d'Hunol-stein; Duveen Brothers, New York; William Randolph Hearst.

EXHIBITIONS
Paris 1880: no. 6

REFERENCES
Müntz 1902: pls. VII and VIII; Ackerman 1940: 187–210; Weibel and Robinson 1955; Weibel and Robinson 1956: 60–63; Detroit 1971: 124; Asselberghs 1974: 23; Brussels 1976: 100

RELATED WORKS
CAT. NOS. 6–8.

DESCRIPTION

There are no inscriptions to corroborate possible identifications. The central figure, wearing armor and wielding a sword, is surely Wrath. Around her are other Vices: Greed who wields a rake; an old woman, perhaps Indolence, who strikes with her crutch; Envy, who swings her staff; and Pleasure, who plays a harp.

In the lower left corner, an unidentified female figure, sits in judgment over a man and three women. Another figure to the right holds an orb. In the two upper left sections, a man and a woman embrace in the court of Vanity, who holds her mirror. Justice with her avenging sword, Greed with a chest of coins, and Gluttony with a golden beaker and platter are present.

In the lower right section, a woman, perhaps Mercy, presents a group of men to the enthroned Christ. The men may represent patriarchs, kings, and prophets of the Old Testament, among whom one would appear to be David with his harp. In the two upper right sections a young man is crowned king in the presence of a large assembly of figures.

[9] *Wrath*

[10] *Triumph of Spring,*
from the "Triumph of the Seasons" Series

ca. 1537–38; designed after the 1537 woodcut by the Flemish
Monogramist A. P.; woven in Bruges
Wool and silk; 9 ft. 2 in. × 13 ft. 8 in. (2.8 × 4 m)
Founders Society Purchase, with contributions from Mrs.
Standish Backus, Mrs. Walter O. Briggs, Mrs. Hugh Dillman,
Mrs. Henry B. Joy, Mrs. Joseph Schlotman, Mr. Edsel B. Ford,
Mr. John S. Newberry, Mr. Robert H. Tannahill, Mr. and Mrs.
Edgar B. Whitcomb (41.40)

PROVENANCE
French & Co., New York.

EXHIBITIONS
Detroit 1958: no. 190.

REFERENCES
Müntz 1878–84: 11; Detroit 1942: 37, 44; Asselberghs 1974: 24, fig.
11; Forti Grazzini 1982: 87, n. 11, fig. 18; Bruges 1987: 216.

RELATED WORKS
The only other extant tapestry from the series is *The Triumph
of Summer,* dated 1538, in the collection of the Bayerische
Hypotheken- und Wechselbank, Munich, and on deposit at the
Bayerisches Nationalmuseum, Munich (inv. L71/45; Bruges 1987:
no. 9).

DESCRIPTION AND INSCRIPTIONS

At the center of a triumphal procession is a chariot,
drawn by doves and lambs, which carries the Goddess of
Flowers (FLORA) and Spring (VER). Guiding the chariot
is the bearded figure of Agriculture (LIBER PATER),
carrying the flowering wreath intended to crown Spring.
Accompanying him is Pan (PAN) playing his reeds,
Orpheus (ORPHEVS) with a stringed instrument, and
Mercury (MERCURI).

Behind the chariot is Apollo (APOLLO) playing
his lyre, followed by the Muses (NOVEM MVSAE), each
with her attributes. Accompanying the procession are
three men bearing standards with MARS, APRILIS, and
MAIVS; pennants at the top of each pole depict the
signs of the Zodiac appropriate for these spring months.

In the background are scenes showing activities
associated with spring. At the extreme left a group pre-
pares the vineyards, indicated by the reference to
D[I]ONYSIVS in the inscription. Next to them are a
couple working in the field, below the inscription
PLEVRESIS. Medieval medicine associated pleurisy with
spring. In the middle ground stand the Three Graces
(CHARITES). In the background behind the chariot is a
hill, where farmers plow. A now-faded inscription next
to the figures refers to Osiris, the Egyptian god who

brought people knowledge of agriculture. A partially
visible inscription (...LENUS) refers to Triptolemus, to
whom the Greek goddess Demeter revealed the art of
growing corn. To the right is a lake; a party in a boat
approaches a chateau on the shore. On one bank stands a
man below the inscription PROFLU VIV SANGVINIS
("flowing forth with blood") a reference to Antique and
medieval medical theory that associated an increase in
blood with the season. Lovers and a musician occupy the
other bank; Cupid (CUPIDO) flies above them. To the
far right is a fountain bearing the inscription FONS CAB/
ALLINUS, a reference to the fountain of the Muses. Next
to the fountain is SA[N]GUINEIS (bloody), referring to
the temperament linked to spring.

At the top is an inscription in Gothic script from
Ovid's *Metamorphoses* (II: 27–28): OVIDI.2.META-
MORPH./VER[QUE] NOVUM STABAT CINCTU[M]
FLORE[N]TE CORONA ("And the new Spring appears,
crowned with a flowery wreath"). The lateral borders
show escutchons near the top bearing on the left the date
1537, and on the right 1538.

Following four lines in Ovid's *Metamorphoses,* the
anonymous Flemish Monogramist A.P. (Hollstein: 12
and FIGS. 10–11) depicted on large woodcuts each season as
an elaborate, triumphant, classical military procession,
embellished with illustrations of the months, the labors,
personifications, and illnesses associated with each season. Among the most important Renaissance tapestries
in the museum's collection, the recently conserved
Triumph of Spring, long considered as made in Germany
or Italy (Ferrara), is a masterwork of tapestry weaving
from the international banking and artistic center of
Bruges (see Forti Grazzini 1982: 87, n. 11; and Delmarcel in
Bruges 1987: 213–17).

Asselberghs (1974: 24) first attributed the *Triumph
of Spring* and the *Triumph of Summer* (on deposit at the
Bayerisches Nationalmuseum, Munich) to a Bruges
tapestry workshop as part of a series of the "Triumph
of the Seasons," the other two of which are unknown.
The floral decoration in the foreground, the rich unusual iron-red dyes of the wool, and especially the
distinctive horizontal borders of putti who straddle
dolphins and hold laurel wreaths, the cornucopia, the
flowers, and the interlaced knots all support this
conclusion. These features on the Detroit and Munich
tapestries can be found on similar **millefleurs** armorial
tapestries documented as woven in Bruges for Matthaus
Lang of Wellenburg between 1520–30 (Fogg Art Museum,

FIG. 10 *Triumph of Spring,* Master A.P. (Flemish), 1537. Woodcut. British Museum, London.

Cambridge) and Paolo Giovio of Rome between 1543–52 (Victoria and Albert Museum, London). Moreover, the decorations of stacked military trophies and putti on the left and right borders, as well as the distinctive red and blue ground, occur on a slightly later tapestry series, "The History of Gombaut and Macée," also woven in Bruges (ibid. and Bruges 1987: nos. 19–26).

Delmarcel discovered (Bruges 1987: 216) that the source of the two extant "Triumph of the Seasons" tapestries is a series of four woodcuts of the "Triumphs of the Four Seasons," dated 1537 and attributed to the anonymous Flemish Monogramist A.P. (Hollstein: 12). He also observed that these woodcuts, which further substantiate the Flemish origin of the tapestries, represent for the first time in northern Renaissance art the allegories of the seasons as a triumphal procession (ibid.). Undoubtedly, they were influenced by earlier Italian visual or literary models, such as paintings or prints by Mantegna or the *Trionfi* of Petrarch.

However, the Bruges weavers transformed the relatively small proportions of the figures and animals in the Master A.P.'s print into more natural, anatomically accurate, muscular images. This is perhaps due to Italian Renaissance influences gained directly or through other weavers in Flemish weaving workshops in Florence and elsewhere in Italy. Also the Bruges weavers have embellished the tapestry further by adding dense fruit-laden foliage, a lush **millefleurs** foreground, and elaborate Roman mannerist-inspired motifs on the richly decorated borders—all characteristics that the woodcut lacks. Curiously, the Detroit tapestry unrolls in the same direction as the 1537 woodcut (Bruges 1987: 217) and was not, as usual, reversed as would have occurred in **low-warp** weaving. The **cartoon** was normally painted in the same direction as the design or *petit patron*; in this case, the woodcut served as the petit patron; on a **low-warp loom** the tapestry image is always reversed, whereas on a **high-warp loom** it is not.

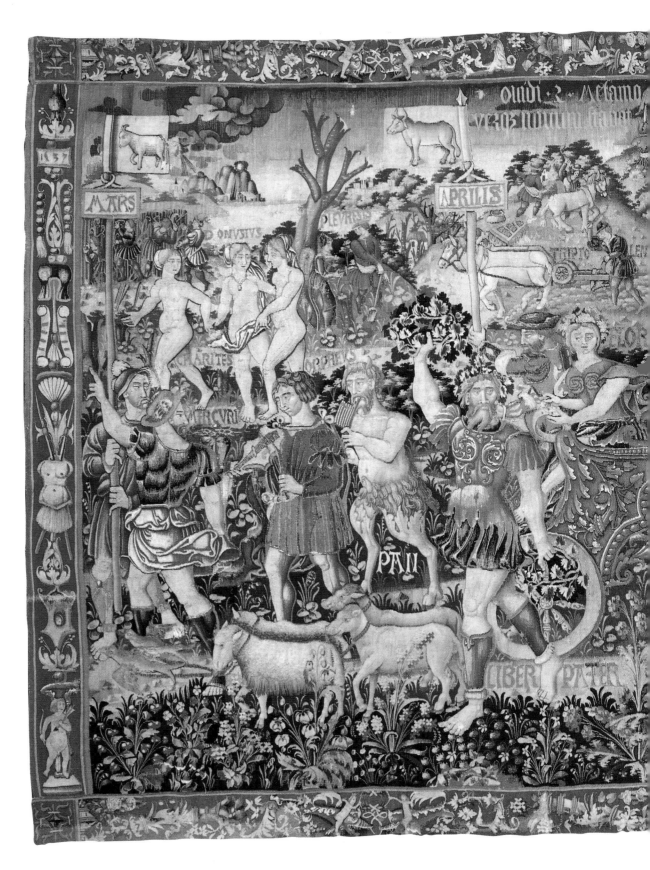

[10] *Triumph of Spring,* from the "Triumph of the Seasons" series

FIG. 11 *Triumph of Summer*, Master A.P. (Flemish), 1537. Woodcut. British Museum, London.

Consequently, Delmarcel (ibid.) has proposed that *The Triumphs of Spring* and *Summer* may represent two of the earliest examples of tapestry weaving on a high-warp loom in Bruges.

Because of an inscription on the *Triumph of Summer*, Lorenz Seelig proposed (Seelig 1976: 32–33) that the Munich tapestry may be somehow related to an exotic subject of the triumph of an African king, *Triumph of the King of Cochin* (depicted in a 1508 woodcut by Hans Burgkmair [1473–1531] in Augsburg). In 1508 a German expedition had explored Cochin, a state on the coast of Malabar in southwest India, and on returning, Burgkmair made woodcuts to represent the tale of the triumphant entry of the Indian king. This woodcut was copied frequently in Germany, France, and the southern Netherlands in the following years in other woodcut editions and in at least one other early sixteenth-century tapestry (Paris, Musée des Arts Africains et Océaniens; see Pochat 1973: 306–09). The Monogramist A.P. probably knew Burgkmair's woodcut, but he transformed it to such a degree that Delmarcel raised the possibility that the inscription on the Munich tapestry may be a restoration (Bruges 1987: 217). The Detroit tapestry lacks the enigmatic inscription, but it shares with the Munich tapestry the same subject celebrating a festive Roman-inspired, and slightly exotic triumphal procession before the inhabitants of a northern European city.   APD

[10] Detail of *Triumph of Spring*

[11] *Antique Battle Scene*

[11] *Antique Battle Scene*
ca. 1615–1622; Brussels
Woven by François Tons (1576–1633)
Mark: Monogram of François Tons in the lower right galloon
Wool and silk; 11 ft. 2 in. × 15 ft. ¼ in. (3.4 × 4.6 m)
Gift of Mrs. Julian Harris in memory of her mother,
Mrs. Henry Stephens (57.146)

PROVENANCE
Duc d'Avaray, Paris; his collection sale, American Art Association, January 22–23, 1915, lot 254 (with three other tapestries from the same set); Mrs. Julian Harris, Nantucket Island, Massachusetts.

EXHIBITIONS
Detroit 1984 (not in catalogue).

REFERENCES
Asselberghs 1974: 25; Asselberghs, Delmarcel, and Garcia Calvo 1985: 102

RELATED WORKS
Six other tapestries, possibly from the same set, are known: three tapestries also in the Duc d'Avaray collection sale, American Art Association, New York, January 22–23, 1915 (lots 252, 253, and 255; the weaver's mark misidentified as that of Jean Raes I); lot 252 later appeared in the Fletcher and Williamson collection sale, American Art Association, New York, January 25, 1918, lot 237; one other was formerly in a California private collection and is now in the Fogg Art Museum, Harvard University, Cambridge, Massachusetts (Parke-Bernet, New York, January 28–29, 1949, lot 415; reproduced in Asselberghs, Delmarcel, and Garcia Calvo 1985: 91, fig. 1); another was formerly in the collection of Mrs. Julian Harris (who identified it as a companion piece) and is now in a private collection in California; and a sixth *The Strategem of Hannibal*, bearing the Brussels city mark, was purchased at the Williamson and Fletcher collection sale, American Art Association, New York, January 25, 1918 (lot 236) by French and Company, New York.

Battle scenes from Greco-Roman history or the Old Testament were popular tapestry subjects in sixteenth- and seventeenth-century Brussels. Inventories record complete sets celebrating the victories of Scipio Africanus, Tarquinius, Hannibal, Alexander, Julius Caesar, and other acclaimed generals. In an era of religious wars and civil unrest, these tapestries served as propaganda for the rulers who commissioned them; envisioning themselves as modern-day heirs of ancient heroes, these patrons exhibited the scenes of valor and military prowess in the tapestries to enhance their own status.

Many individual pieces from these series survive. Unfortunately, the generic character of the battle scenes renders their subjects difficult or impossible to recognize. The Detroit tapestry depicts a fierce battle between a Roman legion (identified by shields decorated with classical ornament and banners emblazoned S.P.Q.R.) and an unidentified enemy. Two protagonists in the combat may offer clues to the subject. In the foreground, a warrior fallen from his horse is protected by a bareheaded youth who separates the two armies at left. The tapestry may depict the Battle of Ticinus, a pivotal conflict early in the Second Punic War (218–201 B.C.) between Carthage and Rome, where a courageous seventeen-year-old Roman soldier Publius Cornelius Scipio (Scipio Africanus) saved his injured father's life.

Another tapestry possibly from the same set, bearing François Tons's mark in the lower right **galloon**, has been traditionally linked to the story of Scipio Africanus (Fogg Art Museum, Cambridge; Asselberghs, Delmarcel, and Garcia Calvo 1985: 91, 102). When the tapestry appeared at auction (New York 1949: lot 415), the catalogue described the subject as Scipio Africanus receiving the keys to the city of New Carthage (captured by Scipio in 209 B.C.) from four kneeling Carthaginian dignitaries. Thomas Campbell related the Detroit tapestry to other Brussels pieces with identical borders (DIA curatorial files, December 15, 1994); two of these, acquired by French and Company in New York in 1918, were inventoried by the dealer as scenes from the story of Scipio Africanus (French and Company archives, Getty Center for the History of Art and the Humanities, Santa Monica). It is difficult to determine whether the Detroit tapestry originally formed a set with these related hangings or whether the subjects have been correctly identified. As a result, the assignment of the Detroit tapestry to a Scipio series remains tentative, albeit tempting.

The story of Scipio Africanus had become a popular tapestry subject during the Renaissance in part because of Petrarch's epic poem *Africa* and vernacular translations of the ancient historian Livy's history of Rome, and also due to the production of a celebrated tapestry series depicting the battles and triumphs of Scipio, designed by Giulio Romano and woven in Brussels in 1532–35 for François I of France (see Paris 1978). Guy Delmarcel recently identified the fragmentary mark in the lower right galloon of the Detroit tapestry as that of the Brussels weaver François (or Frans) Tons (DIA curatorial files, November 24, 1995). Little is known about Tons's activity in Brussels before his departure for Spain in late 1621 or early 1622. In 1616 he delivered to the art dealer Daniel Steurbout tapestry sets depicting the histories of Troy, Scipio Africanus, and Tarquinius (eight pieces each) and, slightly later, a fourth set based on Hannibal's battles (Asselberghs, Delmarcel,

[11] Detail of *Antique Battle Scene*

and Garcia Calvo 1985: 102). The Detroit and Fogg tapestries may have belonged to one of these sets. Certainly the general composition and the floriated border with female allegories of the Virtues and Liberal Arts reveal the refined aesthetic and execution of Brussels tapestry in the second half of the sixteenth century and the early decades of the seventeenth. ?❧ TA

[12] *February,*
from the "Months of Lucas" Series

ca. 1712; Gobelins Manufactory, France
Designed by a Netherlandish artist of the school of Bernard van Orley, known as the Master of the Months of Lucas, ca. 1535; possibly woven in the workshop of Jean Souet (active 1699–1722)
Wool and silk; 10 ft. 6 in. × 10 ft. 6 in. (3.2 × 3.2 m)
Gift of K.T. Keller (66.120)

PROVENANCE
Possibly part of the set ordered by Louis XIV (1638–1715) in 1712 and given in 1717 by Louis XV (1710–74) to the Swedish ambassador to France, Count Erik Axelsson Sparre; I.D. Levy, New York, until 1936; French & Company, New York; acquired by K.T. Keller, Detroit, in 1944.

REFERENCES
Fenaille 1903–23, II: 337–70; Göbel 1928, I: 143–45; Standen 1971: 3–14; Standen 1985, I: 331–60; Bruges 1987: 411–25; Pittsburgh 1987: 149; Arras 1988: 26; Thomas 1990, I: passim.

RELATED WORKS
Seven tapestries from the fifth set, and possibly the same set as the Detroit tapestry, are recorded: four pieces (*May* [with monogram of Jean Souet], *June, July,* and *August*) formerly in the Gaston Menier collection, Paris (Fenaille 1903–23, III: 349; *July* reproduced in Göbel 1928, II: pl. 116), later sold at Galerie Jean Charpentier, Paris, November 24, 1936 (lots 107–10; *August,* marked with the initials of Jean Souet, is now in the Kunstindustrimuseet, Oslo) ; *November,* formerly in the Achille Leclercq collection, sold at Hôtel Drouot, Paris, May 30–June 1, 1904; *January,* recorded in the collection of comtesse Eva Trolle-Bonde, Sweden, in 1928 (Böttiger 1928: no. 97); and *October,* also with Souet's initials, formerly in the Lamm collection, Näsby Castle, Sweden, and sold at the American Art Galleries, New York, February 21–24, 1928, lot 996. A finished drawing for *February,* attributed to the Master of the Months of Lucas, ca. 1535, is in the Devonshire collection, Chatsworth House, Derbyshire (FIG. 12).

The **Gobelins** "Months of Lucas" series is based on a set of sixteenth-century Brussels tapestries recorded in the inventory of the French royal collection from 1684 (no. 8, "fabrique de Bruxelles, dessein de Lucas" [Guiffrey 1885, I: 294]). This celebrated set of Brussels tapestries acquired the name The "Months of Lucas" in the late seventeenth century, when the designer was erroneously thought to be Lucas van Leyden (1494–1533). (For other possible identifications of "Lucas," see Standen 1971: 4.) Stylistic evidence, however, links the designs to an anonymous Netherlandish artist working in the circle of Bernard van Orley in the 1530s. Active in Brussels in the first half of the sixteenth century, van Orley (ca. 1488–1541) played an instrumental role in the transformation of Netherlandish tapestry design by reconciling north-

ern realism with the large-scale figures and deeply receding spaces introduced by Italian Renaissance models, especially Raphael's **cartoons** for the "Acts of the Apostles" tapestry series woven in Brussels in 1516–19. A finished drawing for the cartoon of *February,* is at Chatsworth House (FIG. 12); other drawings for this series survive in various public collections (see Standen 1971: plates 1–7).

First woven in Brussels ca. 1535, the "Months of Lucas" series was copied and adapted at other centers, notably Bruges in the seventeenth century (see Bruges 1987: 411–25) and at the Gobelins manufactory from about 1682 until 1770. The first five sets woven at the Gobelins faithfully reproduced the Brussels originals in the royal collection, including the elaborate wide floral borders with grisailles medallions. The Detroit tapestry may belong to the fifth weaving, made for Louis XIV in the **low-warp** workshop of Jean Souet ca. 1712–15 and given in 1717 by Louis XV to the Swedish ambassador to France, Count Erik Axelsson Sparre. The *February* from the fifth set was woven in 1712. Lacking complete **galloons,** the Detroit tapestry does not bear a weaver's mark and cannot be positively identified with the fifth weaving, although it must predate the sixth of ca. 1722–24. Gobelins designers introduced new elements into the cartoons beginning in 1721 and ultimately provided complete new cartoons for all the months by 1736. Later weavings of *February,* for example, replace the satyr cortege in the landscape at left with a more prosaic scene of woodcutters.

Cycles of the months and seasons were a popular decorative conceit in European art beginning in the Renaissance. The "Months of Lucas" tapestries represent the months by the traditional labors and amusements associated with them in northern Europe: *January* is represented by a New Year's celebration, *February* card playing and tric-trac, *March* fishing, *April* an outdoor concert, *May* archery, *June* sheep-shearing, *July* and *September* the hunt, *August* the harvest, *October* drinking the new vintage, *November* sowing, and *December* ice-skating. In his recent dissertation, Laurent Thomas convincingly suggested that in this series the succession of the months may also be an analogue for the stages in the romantic relationship of a noble couple prominently featured in each cartoon, beginning with their marriage celebration in *January* and concluding with the discovery of the groom's infidelity in *December* (Thomas 1990, I: 40). 〰 TA

[12] *February,* from the "Months of Lucas" Series

FIG. 12 Finished drawing (*petit patron*) for *February*, Master of the Months of Lucas, ca. 1535. Brown wash over black chalk, on brown ground, 37.2 × 47.2 cm. Devonshire Collections, Chatsworth House, Derbyshire, England.

[13] *Winter,*
from the "Seasons of Lucas" Series

Late seventeenth century; Paris or the Gobelins Manufactory, France
Designed by a Netherlandish artist of the school of Bernard van Orley, known as the Master of the Months of Lucas, ca. 1535
Mark: fleurs-de-lys woven in the lower right galloon
Wool and silk; 11 ft. 7 in. × 24 ft. 4 in. (3.5 × 7.4 m)
Gift of Mr. and Mrs. William Fisher (54.440)

PROVENANCE
Probably the tapestry included in an auction, Paris, December 13, 1920 (lot 130); Mr. and Mrs. William Fisher, Detroit.

REFERENCES
New York 1923: 282–83; Ward 1953: 113–19; Standen 1971: 3–14; Standen 1981: 2, 6–7; Standen 1985, I: 322–30; Thomas 1990, II: no. 37.

In a panoramic northern European landscape, dominated by a fanciful Renaissance castle, *Winter* depicts characteristic occupations and diversions of the season: ice skating on a pond, feeding hogs, and gathering wood. A lively drama unfolds as villagers and elegantly attired nobles pair off to skate, apparently oblivious to the fire raging in the town at left. The other tapestries in the "Seasons of Lucas" series also portray rustic pursuits: fishing and gardening in *Spring,* the grain harvest in *Summer,* and the celebration of the new vintage in *Autumn.* A deity appropriate to each season appears in the sky; Aeolus, Greek god of the winds, presides over *Winter* from a cluster of dark storm clouds, brimming with puffing, winged allegories of the winds.

In their overall composition and selection of subjects, the "Seasons of Lucas" resemble the "Months of Lucas" series (see CAT. NO. 12), designed in Brussels about 1535 and copied at the **Gobelins Manufactory** from the late seventeenth century. The "Seasons" **cartoons** likewise reflect the innovative style of early sixteenth-century Brussels tapestries and are securely attributed to the same artist, an anonymous follower of the painter and tapestry designer Bernard Van Orley (ca. 1488–1541), known as the Master of the Months of Lucas. The name "Seasons of Lucas" has no historical foundation but was coined in 1915 by W.G. Thomson in recognition of the clear association between this series and the better-known "Months of Lucas" (New York 1923: 282–83).

Little is known about the production of the "Seasons of Lucas" tapestries in France. All tapestries of this series appear to be of seventeenth- or early eighteenth-century manufacture, although, like the "Months," they apparently copy Brussels designs of ca. 1535 (Standen 1985, I: 322). No sixteenth-century "Seasons of Lucas" tapestries woven in Brussels have been identified, although a complete set must have survived into the seventeenth century to serve as a model. "Seasons" tapestries woven in the mid-seventeenth century in Bruges, probably as variants of the Brussels cartoons, are known, including the *Winter* in the Musée du Louvre, Paris (on deposit at the Musée de l'Hôtel Lallement, Bourges; Arras 1988: no. 23). The Detroit *Winter* is ostensibly a more faithful reproduction of the Brussels original, especially given its use of a typical sixteenth-century Netherlandish border.

As Standen has noted, the color and technique of the Detroit *Winter* and other French pieces suggest that they are Gobelins productions, although the factory records make no mention of the series (Standen 1985, I: 322; DIA curatorial files, 1984). It is possible, however, that the earliest weavings of these designs in France occurred between 1694 and 1699, when the manufactory was closed. The financial burden of the war of the League of Augsburg had exhausted the French treasury by 1694 and royal commissions consequently ceased for a five-year period. The Gobelins weavers continued to work in Paris for private clients and may have unofficially produced the Detroit tapestry during this hiatus. 　　　ba TA

[13] *Winter,* from the "Seasons of Lucas" Series

[14] *Jupiter and Callisto*

ca. 1680; Beauvais Manufactory, France
Wool, silk, and silver thread; 9 ft. 7½ in. × 7 ft. 5¼ in. (2.9 × 2.3 m)
Gift of K.T. Keller (62.135)

PROVENANCE
Made for Vincent Hotman (d. 1683) and Marguerite Colbert (d. 1704), France, ca. 1680; Sale, Victor Rothschild Collection, Christie's, London, April 19–22, 1937 (lot 268, with two other tapestries from this set, see below); private collection, Spain; Paul van Baarn, Paris, ca. 1930s; K.T. Keller, Detroit.

REFERENCES
De la Chenaye-Desbois et Badier 1864, V: 35; Jestaz 1977: 145–51; Jestaz 1979: 187–207.

RELATED WORKS
Two other tapestries from this set, *Apollo and Daphne* (62.134; FIG. 14) and *Venus and Adonis* (62.136; FIG. 13), are also in the collection of the Detroit Institute of Arts.

The story of Jupiter and Callisto appears in Ovid's *Metamorphoses*, a fifteen-volume cyclical poem recounting the transformations of gods and men in Greco-Roman mythology and legend. In this tapestry, Callisto, one of the nymphs of Diana, goddess of the hunt, is approached by Jupiter, who has disguised himself as Diana in order to seduce her. Upon discovering their liaison, Diana banished Callisto, who soon after gave birth to a son. Later Diana changed Callisto into a bear and set her dogs after Callisto. Jupiter saved the nymph by transforming her into the constellation Ursa Major (the Great Bear). Written in the first century A.D., *The Metamorphoses* is composed of tales linked by the common thread of metamorphosis: mythical characters are punished by the gods for their insolence or rewarded for their obedience by a final change into some immortal, astronomical, or natural form.

Rediscovered during the Renaissance, *The Metamorphoses* were translated and widely circulated throughout Europe from the fifteenth to the eighteenth centuries, inspiring the vogue for mythological themes in art, literature, and music. In the late seventeenth and early eighteenth centuries, the **Beauvais Manufactory** wove two discrete series based on the work. In a document of August 19, 1690, the head of the Beauvais factory, Philippe Béhagle, listed as in production sets of both series, differentiated by the size of the figures (Jestaz 1979: 188). Numerous examples of the large-figure series designed by René-Antoine Houasse survive (for example,

FIG. 13 *Venus and Adonis*, Beauvais Manufactory, ca. 1680. Wool, silk, and metallic thread, 9 ft. 7 in. × 7 ft. 6 in. The Detroit Institute of Arts (62.136)

Bennett 1992: 256; Standen 1985, II: 469–72). By contrast, little is known about the second, or small-figure series, including the identity of the designer or the subjects. It is possible that the Detroit tapestry belonged to this second series; the taste for fantasy, the luxuriant foliage derived from Flemish **verdures,** and the prevalence of indigenous and exotic birds in the landscape are all characteristic of Beauvais productions around 1680, the approximate date for the introduction of the small-figure series.

The upper **border** of this tapestry contains the coats of arms of Vincent Hotman (d. 1683), seigneur of Fontenay and Intendant in Touraine, and his wife, Marguerite Colbert (d. 1704), whom he married in 1669 (De la Chenaye-Desbois et Badier 1864, V: 35; Philippe Palasi, DIA curatorial files, 1995). As these tapestries represent the loves of the gods and therefore celebrate love and marriage, it is likely that this set was ordered before Hotman's death in 1683.   TA 🐦

[14] *Jupiter and Callisto*

FIG. 14 *Apollo and Daphne,* Beauvais Manufactory, ca. 1680. Wool, silk, and metallic thread, 9 ft. 8 in. × 11 ft. 8 in. The Detroit Institute of Arts (62.134)

[15] *The Animal Tamers,* from the "Grotesques" Series

ca. 1688–1737
Beauvais Manufactory, France
Designed by Jean-Baptiste Monnoyer (1636–99) and collaborators, ca. 1686–88
Wool and silk; 9 ft. × 12 ft. 9 in. (2.7 × 3.9 m)
Gift of K.T. Keller (62.181)

PROVENANCE
Possibly the tapestry sold at Galerie Georges Petit, Paris, March 8, 1920 (lot 118); French & Company, New York; K.T. Keller, Detroit.

EXHIBITIONS
Detroit 1945: no. 41; Hartford 1951: no. 111; Detroit 1984 (not in catalogue).

REFERENCES
Badin 1909: 56; Göbel 1928, II: 215; Jestaz 1979: 187–208; Standen 1979: 209–13; Standen 1985, II: 441–58; Bennett 1992: 258–65; Adelson 1994: 307–21; Lausanne 1995: 18–20.

Designed before 1689, the **Beauvais** "Grotesques" series manifests the popularity of this style of ornament in late seventeenth- and early eighteenth-century France. Inspired largely by the painted wall decorations at Nero's Domus Aurea, an imperial Roman villa excavated in the 1480s, grotesques are elegant linear decorations organized on a central axis and composed of imaginary architectural structures with scrolling and interlacing foliage and bandwork, often interspersed with classical deities, herms, and fantastic animals. From the 1680s French court designers reinvented the grotesque by transforming the dense patterns favored since the Renaissance into light and whimsical decorations, which they applied to textiles, furniture, book bindings, *boiseries,* and elsewhere.

A document dated 1695 names the designer of the series as Jean-Baptiste Monnoyer (1636–1699), the official flower painter to King Louis XIV (quoted in Standen 1985, II: 422). Beginning in the nineteenth century, however, the Beauvais "Grotesques" **cartoons** were attributed to French court architect and designer Jean I Bérain (1637–

1711), one of the main progenitors of the graceful new grotesque style. Specific motifs, such as the slender columns supporting the airy canopies and the three-bay organization of the wider panels, such as *The Animal Tamers,* are also found in engravings after Bérain's designs published in Paris from 1690 on (for example, see Standen 1979: 210, 211) and leave little doubt that Monnoyer designed the series under Bérain's pervasive influence.

The "Grotesques" series comprises six tapestries: three horizontal pieces depicting a picturesque cast of actors and circus performers, known by the modern titles *The Animal Tamers, The Camel,* and *The Elephant,* and three vertical pieces, known as *The Offering to Bacchus, The Offering to Pan,* and *The Musicians.* The series has no general iconographic or allegorical program but rather serves as a fashionable and purely decorative scheme. Several figures bear a vague resemblance to Commedia dell'Arte characters but cannot be identified with any certainty. A definite theatrical inspiration is, however, revealed by the stagelike settings, including a brilliant purple backdrop in the *Animal Tamers,* and the exotic costumes and masks worn by a number of figures.

On the looms from ca. 1688 until 1737, the "Grotesques" series was the first notable commercial success for the Beauvais manufactory. Several complete sets survive and more than 150 individual pieces from the series are known. *The Animal Tamers,* with only twelve recorded examples, is the rarest of the six subjects (listed in Standen 1985, II: 443–44). The great vogue enjoyed by the "Grotesques" is due, in part, to the dull yellow ground color (called *"tabac d'Espagne"* or *"fond feuille morte"* in period documents), which was also used at the royal Savonnerie carpet manufactory from the mid-1680s. In addition, Beauvais accommodated shifts in taste by weaving the series with three different **borders**: the *chinoiserie,* the simulated gilded frame, and the *bastons rompus* (a fretwork design). The Detroit tapestry had lost its original border by the early twentieth century and cannot, therefore, be given a more precise date on the basis of either the border design or weaver's mark. ❧ TA

[15] *The Animal Tamers*, from the "Grotesques" Series

[16] *Psyche Displaying Her Treasures to Her Sisters,* from the "Psyche" Series

Design ca. 1740, woven 1744–46; Beauvais Manufactory, France
Designed by François Boucher (French, 1703–1770)
Wool and silk; 11 ft. 11 ½ in. × 13 ft. 3 ¾ in. (3.6 × 4 m)
Bequest of Mrs. Horace E. Dodge in memory of her husband
(71.180)

INSCRIPTION
Woven on the step: "F. BOVCHE."

PROVENANCE
Ordered in 1744 by Luigi Reggio e Branciforte (the complete set was delivered in 1746); Reggio e Branciforte family, Naples; Ernest Cronier, Paris; his collection sale, Galerie Georges Petit, Paris, December 4–5, 1905, lot 164; George Jay Gould (d. 1923), Lakewood, New Jersey; Duveen Brothers, New York; acquired by Anna Thomson Dodge in 1932.

REFERENCES
Macfall 1908: 136; Detroit 1933: n.p.; Detroit 1939, I: n.p.; *Art Quarterly* 1971: 500, 504; Winokur 1971: 48–49; *Gazette des Beaux-Arts* 1972: 96, fig. 338; Hiesinger 1976: 7–23; Forti Grazzini 1993, II: 393, 492; Hawley in Dell et al. 1996: no. 37 (see for a complete list of references).

Psyche Displaying Her Treasures illustrates an episode from the fable of Psyche, introduced by the Roman poet Apuleius in the *Golden Ass* (books 4–6) of the 2nd century A.D. As the story begins, Venus, envious of the mortal Psyche's beauty, bids her son Cupid to arrange Psyche's marriage to a monster. However, upon seeing Psyche, Cupid fell in love with her and secretly brought her to his palace, where he visited her only at night so as not to be recognized. Curious about her lover's identity and urged on by her jealous sisters, Psyche one night approached Cupid's bed with an oil lamp; a drop of hot oil fell on Cupid's shoulder and woke him. He fled in anger, the palace vanished, and Psyche began to wander the earth in search of her lover, performing difficult tasks set out by Venus to prove her devotion. Jupiter, heeding Cupid's entreaties, eventually took pity on Psyche and brought her to Mount Olympus for a reunion with Cupid.

Commissioned by Louis XV in November 1737, the "Story of Psyche" was the second major series designed by François Boucher for the **Beauvais Manufactory.** First recorded on the looms in 1741, the series remained in production for thirty years. Only ten or twelve complete sets were ordered, although many versions of each scene were executed individually or in smaller sets. The series comprised five tapestries: *The Arrival at Cupid's Palace, The Toilet of Psyche, Psyche Displaying Her Treasures to Her Sisters, The Abandonment,* and *The Basketweaver,* the last recounting the rescue of the despondent Psyche by a rustic basketmaker and his daughters. The Detroit tapestry belongs to a complete set ordered in 1744 by the Spanish ambassador to France; Philippe Palasi identified the coats of arms in the upper border as those of ambassador Luigi Reggio e Branciforte (ambassador to France 1741–46; d. 1758) and his wife Caterina Gravina (DIA curatorial files, 1992). *The Abandonment* and *The Basketweaver,* bearing identical arms, were also sold from the collection of Ernest Cronier, Paris, in 1905 (Paris 1905: lot 165 and 1666); and again from a private collection in 1991 (Monaco 1991: lots 563 and 564).

The Psyche legend enjoyed great popularity in French art from the time of the Renaissance. Boucher nonetheless created **cartoons** of great originality, depicting uncommon episodes and finding inspiration in late-seventeenth-century versions of the story by the playwright Molière and the fabulist La Fontaine. The third cartoon, *Psyche Displaying Her Treasures,* is based on La Fontaine's account of 1669:

> One could see a dozen nymphs around
> a dressing table… gathered in abundance
> were…vessels and baths of chased gold,
> articles of luxury… elsewhere were piles
> of jewels, ornaments and chains of precious
> stones, bracelets, necklaces, and other
> Cytherian treasures. They showed strings
> of pearls; they spread out costumes glitter-
> ing with diamonds… (Hiesinger 1976: 15).

As evident in this series, the fable of Psyche had lost its moralizing message by the mid-eighteenth century and become, in Diderot's words, a "charming fairy tale" (Hiesinger 1976: 20).   ❧ **TA**

[16] *Psyche Displaying Her Treasures to Her Sisters,* from the "Psyche" Series

[17] *Four Tapestry Screen Panels*

ca. 1755–65; Gobelins Manufactory, France
After designs by François Boucher (French, 1703–70)
Wool and silk; Each panel: 2 ft. 6¼ in. × 1 ft. 6⅞ in. (82 × 48 cm)
Bequest of Mrs. Horace E. Dodge in memory of her husband
(71.181)

PROVENANCE
Charles Wertheimer, London; Herbert Stern; Baron Michelham, before 1912; Duveen Brothers, New York; acquired by Anna Thomson Dodge, 1935.

REFERENCES
Molinier 1902: 19 (as Beauvais); Fenaille 1903–23, IV: 407; London 1912: 42; Detroit 1939, I: n.p.; Standen 1994: 111–33; Hawley in Dell et al. 1996: no. 38 (see for a complete list of references).

RELATED WORKS
A set of six armchairs, upholstered with related Gobelins tapestry covers depicting Boucher's "Country Children," were also formerly in the Charles Wertheimer collection, London, ca. 1900 (sold at Hôtel Drouot, Paris, April 26, 1900; Fenaille 1903–23, IV: 406–07).

Among the decorations most frequently found on surviving **Gobelins** upholsteries are the so-called Country Children after François Boucher (Standen 1994: 111–12). As examples of this type, each panel of the Detroit screen depicts a child, aged about seven to ten years, engaged in a pleasurable rustic pursuit: from left to right, weaving a floral wreath, tying a ribbon around the neck of a lamb, playing bagpipes, and eating from a bowl instead of churning butter. The attribution of the designs to Boucher is based on inscriptions on contemporary engravings for each subject (see Hawley in Dell et al. 1996: no. 38). Boucher also provided the Gobelins manufactory with other, more characteristic designs for tapestry— such as putti in clouds and child Allegories of the Arts—though these are far less common on Gobelins upholsteries than the "Country Children." The Detroit panels may have been woven in the workshop of the Gobelins weaver Jacques Neilson (active 1749–88), who specialized in furnishing upholsteries of this type (see Langer and Ottomeyer 1995: no. 41, for example).

The "Country Children" also appeared in other media in the mid-eighteenth century, especially as ceramic sculpture and as painted decoration on Vincennes (and later Sèvres) porcelain. To the eighteenth century, the "Country Children" symbolized the simple virtues of country life and childhood, celebrated in Enlightenment literature and heralding new attitudes toward childhood and family life.

Unlike its rival establishment at **Beauvais**, the Gobelins manufactory did not customarily make tapestry upholstery to accompany wall hangings. The factory's eighteenth-century records mention only thirty-five sets of furniture tapestry and few covers for armchairs, settees, and fire screens survive (Watson 1961: 166). A royal enterprise, the Gobelins supplied sets of furniture covers to Louis XV, Madame de Pompadour, and her brother the marquis de Marigny in the 1750s and 1760s, though the majority of upholstery sets were made for private patrons, particularly the English nobility and gentry (Standen 1994: 111). Unfortunately, factory records are not complete and do not list all private commissions, thereby making it impossible to determine the number of upholstery sets actually woven during the eighteenth century.

Four mid-eighteenth-century tapestry panels were mounted in a later, Régence-style frame to create this tall, folding screen (*paravent*). The original function of the panels is a matter of conjecture, although they were most likely made for a screen. A number of similar panels of comparable dimension and subject survive in small, eighteenth-century fire screens (*écrans*). An art dealer or collector may have assembled the *paravent* in the nineteenth century using tapestry panels salvaged from four eighteenth-century fire screens (Hawley in Dell et al. 1996: 38). Low, folding screens of two to four panels, also placed in front of a fireplace, and *paravents,* though rarer, represent other possible applications.   TA

[17] *Four Tapestry Screen Panels*

[18] *Pair of Armchairs* (fauteuils à la reine)
with Tapestry Upholstery

ca. 1780–85;
Wool and silk upholstery woven at the Beauvais
Manufactory, France
Chairs stamped by Georges Jacob (French, 1739–1814)
Gilded beechwood; 35⅞ × 25¼ × 25½ in. (91 × 64 × 65 cm)
Bequest of Mrs. Horace E. Dodge in memory of her husband
(71.182, 71.183)

PROVENANCE

Sale, Madame Billout-Desmarets collection, Galerie Georges
Petit, Paris, June 1, 1923, lot 20 (to Vagliano); André J. Seligman,
Paris; acquired by Anna Thomson Dodge through L. Alavoine,
New York, 1932.

REFERENCES

Paris 1932: lot 20; *Gazette des Beaux-Arts* 1972: 93, fig. 325;
Ledoux-Lebard 1975: 36–38; Dell in Dell et al. 1996: no. 19.

RELATED WORKS

A suite of six armchairs having nearly identical tapestry covers,
documented as late eighteenth-century Beauvais, is in the
Grand Trianon, Versailles (Ledoux-Lebard 1975: 36–38).

All the principal French tapestry manufactories—
including **Aubusson, Beauvais,** and **Gobelins**—wove
furniture covers during the eighteenth century. The total
output was nevertheless comparatively small, estimated
at approximately six hundred sets of covers for the period
1715 to 1789 (Watson 1961: 1966). Of the factories, Beauvais
was the most prolific producer of high-quality upholsteries for a fashionable Parisian clientele. Factory records for
the years 1725 to 1793 list 228 orders for suites of furniture,
including canapés, chairs, beds, screens, bed hangings,
and stools, totaling more than 1700 individual pieces (see
Badin 1909: 67–75 for complete listing). Orders ranged in
size from a cover for a single canapé or screen to complete bedhangings with twelve matching chairs.

This pair of gilded armchairs belongs to a set of six,
stamped by the Parisian furniture maker Georges Jacob
(1734–1814) and upholstered with identical Beauvais
tapestry panels of the early 1780s. Given their ample
proportions and square backs, the frames are ideally
suited to tapestry upholsteries. The back panels depict
baskets of flowers, hanging by tasseled ropes from ara-
besque scrolls and floral garlands; below the baskets are
olive branches, symbolizing peace. On the seat covers are
trophies of musical instruments, Apollo's lyre, and
Cupid's bow and quiver, emblems of love. When the set
appeared at auction in 1923, the catalogue described the
chairs as having been reupholstered (Paris 1923: lot 20).
Certainly, eighteenth-century covers were often salvaged
and refit on other frames, especially during the early
twentieth century when the vogue for tapestry-covered
furniture was at its height. However, the covers of the
Detroit chairs appear to have been designed for them, and
the majority of chairs of this model have tapestry covers
of either Aubusson or Beauvais manufacture (Dell in Dell
et al. 1996: no. 19).

In the late seventeenth century, Beauvais had begun
the lucrative practice of weaving upholstery to accompany its wall hangings. Of the thirty-eight different
upholstery designs woven during the eighteenth century,
floral panels such as those on the Detroit chairs were
ordered most frequently. The Detroit tapestries nonetheless represent a rare variation of this type. Their
attribution to Beauvais is confirmed by six other armchairs with documented upholsteries (Dell in Dell et al.
1996: no. 19). Those six chairs belonged to a set of thirty-
three pieces made by the Paris firm Jacob-Desmalter for
the Petit Trianon, Versailles, in 1805 and now mostly
preserved in the Grand Trianon (Ledoux-Lebard 1975:
36–38). The covers on the Trianon armchairs are identical in every aspect to those on the Detroit chairs, except
for the use of a brown **border**, rather than green, on the
back panels. ❧ TA

[18] *One of a Pair of Armchairs* (fauteuils à la reine) *with Tapestry Upholstery*

[19] *The Passing of Venus*

[19] *The Passing of Venus*

Woven ca. 1922–26; Morris and Company, Merton Abbey
Tapestry Works, Surrey, England
Woven by Percy Sheldrick (English, active 1922–39) under the
supervision of J. Henry Dearle (English, active 1887–1932)
Designed by Edward Coley Burne-Jones (English, 1833–1898)
1872–1890s
Wool and silk; 8 ft. 11 ft. × 19 ft. 3 in. (2.7 × 5.9 m)
Gift of George G. Booth (27.152)

INSCRIPTIONS

In two scrolls in the upper border: *Comment des jeunes colom-
beaux/En ung char qui fut riche et beau/Mainent Venus en lost
a'Amours/pour lui faire hatif secours* ("How some young doves
pull Venus in a chariot that was rich and beautiful to the group
of loves in order to help them without delay")

MARKS

On border: *Merton Abbey* and *P.S.* [Percy Sheldrick]

PROVENANCE

Commissioned by George G. Booth for the Detroit Institute of
Arts in 1922.

EXHIBITIONS

Wilmington 1976: no. 4–63; Detroit 1976: no. 147; Detroit 1978:
no. 17; Providence 1979: no. 33; Katonah 1992: unnumbered;
Detroit 1993: not in catalogue.

REFERENCES

Burne-Jones 1900: 162; *Art Journal* 1908: 182; Vallance 1908: 16,
18; *The Times,* London 1923; Marillier 1927: 21–22, 35; Weibel
1927: 78; Zick 1972: 307–48; Parry 1975: 328; *Antiques* 1978: 392;
Fairclough and Leary 1981: 63, 78 n. 28, 111; Parry 1983: 117–19,
125; Parry 1983a: 16–22; Standen 1985, II: no. 135; Raynor 1992;
Menz 1994: 68; Detroit 1995: 233; Joubert, Lefébure, and
Bertrand 1995: 318-20, 352.

RELATED WORKS

A fragment showing the head of a female figure at right is in the
Metropolitan Museum of Art, New York (Boyce 1910: 138; Standen
1985, II: no. 135). The initial conception of *Venus* derives from the
background decoration seen in Edward Burne-Jones's painting of
Laus Veneris (Lang Art Gallery in Newcastle-upon-Tyne) of 1872–
75 (Marillier 1927: 21–22; Parry 1975: 328). A study for this tapestry,
by Burne-Jones, is in the Metropolitan Museum of Art, New York
(FIG. 15). A preparatory pencil sketch from 1877 for the figure of the
queen, Sappho, is in the Art Gallery of South Australia, Adelaide
(Parry 1983: 118; Menz 1994: 68, no.19). A three-dimensional model
in wood, metal, and wax representing the metal cage of the seated
Venus was made after the Burne-Jones's study, at his request, so
he and J. Henry Dearle, artistic director of Merton Abbey, could
choose the best angle and produce related drawings. A photograph
and drawings of this seated Venus and chariot model survive; the
latter is in the Fogg Art Museum (Zick 1972: 320–21, fig. 9, 11, and
Parry 1983: 187 n. 51). Burne-Jones's gouache study (FIG. 15) and
Dearle's drawing for *The Passing of Venus* tapestry were exhibited
at the Arts and Crafts Society exhibition in London in 1899 (Fairclough and Leary 1981: 111). Two work plans for the weaving of the
Detroit tapestry and its border drawn by Percy Sheldrick are in the
collection of Sanford and Helen Berger, Carmel, California.

William Morris, leader of the nineteenth-century
English Arts and Crafts movement, reacted vehemently
against the methods he witnessed at the **Gobelins**
tapestry manufactory in Paris and the prevalent nineteenth-century French tradition of producing tapestries
copied directly from oil paintings. Morris wrote, "It
would be a mild word to say what they [the Gobelins]
do is worthless." He believed all recent weavings by the
Gobelins, **Beauvais,** and **Aubusson** manufactories and
the French-inspired Royal Windsor Tapestry Works had
changed the art of tapestry to an "upholsterer's toy"
(Parry 1975: 324–25: excerpted from Morris's *The Lesser
Arts of Life: Arts and Crafts Essay,* 1882).

The Passing of Venus, designed by Edward Burne-
Jones between 1877 and the 1890s for William Morris and
Company's tapestry studio at **Merton Abbey,** is the largest
and most elaborate tapestry the firm ever produced.
Venus enters from the left in a chariot drawn by doves.
She oversees Eros who draws his bow, while twelve maid-
ens, one of whom has already fallen under his foot, huddle
around Sappho, the celebrated ancient Greek woman
poet, who stands regally in a white robe and blue mantle
on the dais at the right. The theme derives from a conflation
of *Le Romaunt de la Rose,* the thirteenth-century French
poem of courtly love (Marillier 1927: 21), and the theme of
Love Triumphant from Petrarch's *Trionfi* (Zick 1972: 332–
339). Other literary sources also inspired the subject, like
Chaucer's translation of the *Romance of the Rose* (Parry
1983: 117) and Algernon Charles Swindburne's nineteenth-
century romantic story of Sappho (Zick 1972: 332–339).
The composition relates to Florentine Renaissance paintings, such as Botticelli's *Primavera* (Galleria degli Uffizi,
Florence) and Signorelli's *Triumph of Chastity* (National
Gallery, London).

Although Burne-Jones worked on the ***petit patron***
for this tapestry (FIG. 15) until his death in 1898 (Standen
1985, II: no. 135), J. Henry Dearle, the artistic director of
Merton Abbey, oversaw production of the tapestry
design, supervised the weavers, and wove parts of the
tapestry. Dearle also added ornament and completed the
design for the tapestry after Burne-Jones' death, according to Dearle's letter of 1926 to Detroit collector and
businessman George G. Booth (Parry 1983: 118).

The tapestry was probably intended to form part of
a narrative cycle with the *Pilgrim in the Garden,* also
known as *The Heart of the Rose* (Badisches Landesmuseum,
Karlsruhe) and *Love and the Pilgrim* (Birmingham
Museum and Art Gallery, England). These smaller tapestries after Burne-Jones designs were woven at Merton
Abbey between 1901 and 1909. *The Passing of Venus* was
first woven in 1901–07, with an acanthus leaf rather than

FIG. 15 Sketch for *The Passing of Venus*, 1898, Edward Coley Burne-Jones (English, 1833-1898), gouache, 16 $\frac{1}{16}$ × 38 $\frac{11}{16}$ in. The Metropolitan Museum of Art, Rogers Fund (62.167).

a floral border and without an inscription. The piece was shown at the New Gallery Summer Exhibition, London, in 1908. The work was lent to the British section of the Brussels Exposition of 1910, where it was destroyed by fire. What may be a fragment from this piece (or perhaps a copy from 1913) survives in the Metropolitan Museum of Art (Standen 1985, II: 745, no 135).

On March 30, 1909, Morris and Company offered Booth *The Passing of Venus* panel at the price of 1,500 pounds, calling it "in many respects the finest piece which has been made on the Merton Abbey Looms" (Parry 1983a: 18). Although this first weaving of *The Passing of Venus* was to perish, the lack of a prompt reply from Booth, then president of the *Detroit News,* led to eventual good fortune for tapestry collecting and weaving programs in Michigan. The second weaving of the *Passing of Venus* was commissioned by Booth for 2,000 pounds in 1922 and donated in 1927 to the Detroit Institute of Arts. It was woven between 1922 and 1926 by master-weaver Percy Sheldrick (Parry 1983: 107) under the supervision of J. Henry Dearle. To maintain the high standards Booth sought for this "museum" commission, he requested the use of rare natural vegetable dyes. Harry Currie Marillier, a director of the Morris firm, wrote on May 11, 1921:

> It is the last great tapestry which we shall loom-make in which the old vegetable dyes used by the Flemish weavers can be employed, because these dyes are no longer obtainable. Madder, which is the chief of them, has gone completely out of cultivation for dyeing and there seems no pros-

pect of it ever being revived as few people other than ourselves were using it. We do not find alizarin substitute nearly so fine in colour or so good. In considering the choice of a Museum tapestry, I should consider this a very important point. (Parry 1983a: 20)

Booth specified other modifications to the original design as well: a larger and "more suitable" decorative floral border was requested; the iron cage surrounding Venus was reduced in color intensity "to make it less prominent"; and Booth turned down the first proposed inscription from the firm, which contained the overly-businesslike word "company" (Parry 1983a: 20–23). The final inscription, proposed by Dearle to Booth, was taken from the French medieval poem *Le Romaunt de la Rose* (correspondence, J.H. Dearle to G. Booth, 20 December 1922, Cranbrook Archives).

Booth's commission of the *Passing of Venus* ended an era. With this and other smaller tapestries commissioned from Morris and Company for Cranbrook, Booth nearly single-handedly enabled this important British tapestry firm to remain solvent and in production another fifteen years until it closed finally on March 12, 1940. ❧ APD

FIG. 16 Detail from *The Passing of Venus* (CAT. NO. 19)

CHECKLIST
of European Tapestries in the Detroit Institute of Arts

European tapestries not included in this exhibition are listed here under the country or region of manufacture, in order of their accession into the Detroit Institute of Arts collection.

ENGLAND

Fragment: Flowers, 17th century
15½ × 31 in. (39.4 × 78.7 cm)
Gift of Mrs. E.S. Fechimer; 47.133

Possibly from the workshop of Stephen de May at the Mortlake Manufactory
Alpheus and Arethusa, late 17th century
5 ft. 11 in. × 8 ft. 9 in. (1.8 × 2.6 m)
Gift of Clarence H. Booth; 49.415

Bibliography: Marillier 1930: 82; Göbel 1934, II: 203–206; Hefford 1983: 106, fig. 12.

SOUTHERN NETHERLANDS

Brussels
Cartoon by Pieter Coecke van Aelst
Saint Paul before Porcius Festus, King Herod Agrippa and His Sister Berenice, from the "Saint Paul" *Series,* ca. 1535–40
12 ft. × 23 ft. 3 in. (3.7 × 7 m)
Founders Society Purchase; 24.29

Bibliography: Friedländer 1917: 73–94, ill.; Walther 1924: 4–6, ill.; Baldass 1924: [2–6], ill.; Baldass 1924a: 45, ill.; Marilier 1966: 310; Cavallo 1967, I: 98–103; Worcester 1969: 45–48, ill.; Asselberghs 1974: 24; Schloss Halbturn 1981: 37–54.

Verdure, ca. 1700
Approx. 9 ft. × 4 ft. (2.7 × 1.2 m)
City of Detroit Purchase; 27.185

Verdure, ca. 1700
Approx. 9 ft. × 4 ft. (2.7 × 1.2 m)
City of Detroit Purchase; 27.186

Antwerp, Pieter Wauters
Cartoon by Pieter Spierincx
The Riding School: Curvetting to the Right, from the "Manège" *Series,* ca. 1670
13 ft. 5 in. × 19 ft. 3 in. (4.1 × 5.8 m)
Gift of Marion Jarves Alger in memory of her husband, Russell A. Alger; 35.2

Bibliography: Göbel 1923, I: 456; Weibel 1935: 44–47, ill.; Duverger 1959: 123, 163–65; Asselberghs 1974: 25.

Antwerp, Pieter Wauters
Cartoon by Pieter Spierincx
The Riding School: The Trot, from the "Manège" *Series,* ca. 1670
13 ft. 4 in. × 15 ft. 4 in. (4 × 4.6 m)
Gift of Marion Jarves Alger in memory of her husband, Russell A. Alger; 35.3

Bibliography: Göbel 1923, I: 456; Weibel 1935: 44–47, ill.; Duverger 1959: 123, 163–65; Asselberghs 1974: 25.

Brussels
Scene of Judgment, early 16th century
12 ft. 2 in. × 1 ft. 3 in. (3.7 × 3.1 m)
By exchange from Edsel B. Ford and General Membership Fund; 43.29

Bibliography: Weibel 1943: 79–81; Asselberghs 1974: 23.

Brussels
Scene from Roman History: The Tribute, 17th century
10 ft. 11 in. × 12 ft. 7 in. (3.3 × 3.8 m)
Gift of Virginia Booth Vogel and John Lord Booth; 43.52

Bibliography: Asselberghs 1974: 25.

Fragment of a Horizontal Border, 17th century
3 ft. 11 in. × 10 in. (118 × 27.3 cm)
Gift of Robert H. Tannahill; 44.155

Two Fragments of Vertical Borders: The Prodigal Son Taking Leave of His Father and The Prodigal Son as a Swineherd, 17th century
Each 5 ft. 1 in. × 1 ft. 8 in. (154.9 × 49.5 cm)
Gift of Mrs. Ernest Kanzler; 44.157.a-b

Fragment of a Horizontal Border: Three Theological Virtues, Faith, Charity, and Hope, second half 16th century
3 ft. 9 in. × 8 ft. 6 in. (1.1 × 2.6 m)
Gift of K.T. Keller; 46.325

Exhibited: Detroit 1991: no. 22.

Medallion Fragment of a Border: Justice, late 16th century
2 ft. 7 in. × 1 ft. 11 in. (77.5 × 58.4 cm)
Gift of K.T. Keller; 46.327

Brussels
Fragment of a Large Tapestry: Group of Men, ca. 1525
5 ft. 10 in. × 7 ft. 3 in. (1.8 × 2.2 m)
Gift of Hans Arnhold; 46.358

Brussels, Franz Geubels
Landscape with Castle and Animals, ca. 1560
11 ft. 6 in. × 10 ft. 4 in. (3.5 × 3.2 m)
Founders Society Purchase and funds from Oscar Webber; 47.40

Bibliography: Weibel 1947a: 6–10, ill.; Knowlton 1956: 131–144; Duverger 1969: 174–78, fig. 20; Asselberghs 1974: 25.

Brussels, Jacob Geubels
Vertumnus and Pomona,
late 16th century
11 ft. 9 in. × 10 ft. 6 in. (3.6 × 3.2 m)
Founders Society Purchase and funds
from Richard Webber; 47.41

Bibliography: Göbel 1923, I: 322; Weibel
1947a: 6–10, ill.; Asselberghs 1974: 25.
Exhibited: Detroit 1945: no. 24;
Hartford 1951: no. 92.

Border Fragment: Mermaid,
late 16th century
22 × 19 ¾ in. (55.9 × 50.2 cm)
Gift of Mrs. E. S. Fechimer; 47.334

Panel: Verdure with Parrot, 19th century
2 ft. 8 in. × 2 ft. 5 in. (81.9 × 73 cm)
Gift of Mrs. E. S. Fechimer; 47.335

Fragment: Birds, 18th century
11 × 34 ½ in. (27.9 × 87.6 cm)
Gift of Mrs. E. S. Fechimer; 47.336

Tournai
After Bernard van Orley
Fragment: The Wolf Hunt, ca. 1525
8 ft. 7 in. × 7 ft. (2.6 × 2.1 m)
Gift of K.T. Keller; 47.401

Bibliography: Asselberghs 1974: 24.
Exhibited: Tournai 1970: no. 26.

Tournai
Triumph of Gluttony, ca. 1510
13 ft. 4 in. × 17 ft. 3 in. (4 × 5.2 m)
Gift of Mrs. Sidney D. Waldon in memory
of Colonel Sidney Dunn Waldon; 50.60

Bibliography: Cavallo 1952: 86–89, ill.;
Asselberghs 1974: 23.

Brussels
Venus and Mars Surprised by Vulcan,
mid-16th century
12 ft. × 13 ft. 4 in. (3.7 × 4 m)
Gift of John Lord Booth and
Virginia Booth Vogel; 51.60

Bibliography: Asselberghs 1974: 25.

Brussels, Peter van den Hecke
Cartoon by Jan van Orley
and Augustin Coppens
Venus Hears of Cupid's Burn, from the
"Psyche" *Series,* 1715–25
10 ft. × 12 ft. 11 in. (3 × 3.8 m)
Gift of Mr. and Mrs. William A. Fisher;
52.319

Bibliography: Göbel 1923, I: 361, 597, n.
110; Asselberghs 1974: 25; Vianden 1995:
no. 21; Reyniès 1995: 209–20.

Two Vertical Borders: The Four Quarters
of the World, 17th century
Overall 8 ft. 3 in. × 6 ft. 3 in. (2.5 × 1.9 m)
Gift of Albert Kahn Associated
Architects and Engineers, Inc.; 53.462

Verdure, 18th century
9 ft. × 9 ft. 8 in. (2.7 × 2.9 m)
Gift of Robert P. Scherer; 54.295

Brussels
Venus and Adonis, mid-16th century
9 ft. 8 in. × 12 ft. (2.9 × 3.6 m)
Gift of Mr. and Mrs. Henry E. Bodman;
55.228

Bibliography: Asselberghs 1974: 25.

Oudenarde
Verdure: Landscape with Animals
and Birds, late 16th century
9 ft. 9 in. × 11 ft. 11 in. (3.0 × 3.6 m)
Gift of Mrs. Henry P. Williams; 56.116

Bibliography: Weibel 1956: 12–13, ill.

Attributed to Brussels
Landscape with Figures, early 17th century
10 ft. 8 in. x 8 ft. 6 in. (3.2 x 2.6 m)
Gift of Mrs. William E. Scripps; 56.294

Pastoral Scene: Musicians and Dancers
in a Landscape, 18th century
9 ft. 8 in. × 12 ft. 1 in. (2.9 × 3.7 m)
Gift of Mrs. William E. Scripps; 56.295

Brussels, Urbain Leyniers
After Jan van Orley and Augustin Coppens
Don Quixote and the Windmills,
early 18th century
11 ft. × 8 ft. 5 in. (3.3 × 2.6 m)
Bequest of Hettie B. Speck, 1950; 61.395

Bibliography: Göbel 1923, I: 342;
Asselberghs 1974: 25.

Oudenarde
Rome Crowned by Victory, from the
"History of Rome" *Series,*
third quarter 17th century
11 ft. 4 in. × 8 ft. 4 in. (3.4 × 2.5 m)
Bequest of Hettie B. Speck, 1950; 61.396
Bibliography: Asselberghs 1974: 25.

Brussels
After David Teniers the Younger
Five Peasants Smoking and Drinking
Around a Table, first half 18th century
9 ft. 2 in. × 5 ft. 11 in. (2.8 × 1.8 m)
Gift of Howard Young; 63.137

Brussels, Franz van den Hecke
Roman Triumph, mid-17th century
10 ft. 5 in. × 18 ft. 4 in. (3.2 × 5.6 m)
Bequest of Mrs. Theodore Bargman;
65.77

Attributed to Brussels
Probably after David Teniers the Younger
Entrefenêtre, 18th century
9 ft. 1 in. × 4 ft. 3 in. (2.8 × 1.3 m)
Gift of Mr. and Mrs. Robert W. Scripps
and Mr. and Mrs. R. M. Spitzley; 68.116

Brussels
Allegorical Landscape with Three Muses,
late 17th-early 18th century
11 ft. 3 in. × 8 ft. 8 in. (3.4 × 2.6 m)
Bequest of Dollie May Fisher; 68.346

Fragment: Bishop Saint, ca. 1490
6 ft. 10 in. × 2 ft. 5 in. (207 × 73.7 cm)
Gift of Mrs. C.S. Mott; 74.299

Verdure Tapestry: Landscape with a
Waterbird, mid-17th century
8 ft. 2 in. × 5 ft. 6 in. (2.5 × 1.6 m)
Gift of Mr. and Mrs. T. Chalmers Curtis
in memory of George Lewis Curtis; F68.1

FRANCE

Aubusson
After Jean-Joseph Dumons
and Nicolas-Jacques Julliard
The Honeymoon,
second half 18th century
8 ft. 8 in. × 12 ft. (2.6 × 3.7 m)
Gift of Charles Stinchfield; 14.6

Aubusson
The Hunters' Breakfast, ca. 1770
8 ft. 6 in. × 5 ft. 7 in. (2.6 × 1.7 m)
Gift of Lillian Henkel Haass; 32.17

Bibliography: Weibel 1932: 99, ill.

Paris, Alexandre de Comans
After Simon Vouet
Rinaldo Carried Off by Armida,
from the "Rinaldo and Armida" *Series,*
second quarter 17th century
10 ft. × 13 ft. (3 × 3.4 m)
Gift of Fred Wardell; 40.135

Bibliography: Fenaille 1903-23, I: 319-34;
Göbel 1928, I: 88-91.

Beauvais Manufactory
Fragment of a Vertical Border,
late 17th-early 18th century
3 ft. 5 in. × 9 in. (104.1 × 22.9 cm)
Gift of Robert H. Tannahill; 44.154

Aubusson or provincial France,
possibly the workshop of Jacques de
Claravaux at Aubusson
Taking of Briseis from the Tent of Achilles,
second half 17th century
10 ft. 8 in. × 14 ft. (3.3 × 4.3 m)
Gift of K.T. Keller; 44.214

Bibliography: Göbel 1928, I: 526-27;
Brussels 1977: 103.

Gobelins Manufactory
Fragment of the Upper Border from a
Tapestry of the "Mythological Subjects
after Raphael" *Series,* ca. 1687-91
Designed by Jean Lemoine de Lorrain
(1638-1713), Claude-Guy Hallé (1652-
1736), and Bon Boulogne (1649-1717)
Probably from *The Marriage of Cupid*
and Psyche woven in the workshop of
Jean Jans the Younger
2 ft. × 6 ft. 2 in. (61.1 × 186.7 cm)
Gift of K.T. Keller; 46.251

Bibliography: Fenaille 1903-23, II: 246-
78; Göbel 1928, I: 138-40; Weibel 1947:
62, ill.; Standen 1964: 43-57; Ypersele de
Strihou 1970: 282, 287-89, 296-300, 302,
305, 306; Standen 1985, I: 285-86, 291-93.

Gobelins Manufactory
Fragment: Verdure, 18th century
10 × 31 in. (25.4 × 78.7 cm)
Gift of Mrs. E.S. Fechimer; 47.337

Paris, Alexandre de Comans
After a set of paintings by Simon Vouet
for the Hôtel de Buillon, Paris,
ca. 1634-35
Carlo and Ubaldo Spy on the Lovers,
from the "Rinaldo and Armida" *Series,*
second quarter 17th century
13 ft. 9 in. × 16 ft. 3 in. (3.6 × 5.0 m)
Bequest of Anna E. Kresge; 47.402

Bibliography: Weibel 1950: 4, ill.;
Versailles 1967: 30.

Lille, probably the workshop
of Guillaume Werniers
In the style of David Teniers
the Younger (1610-94)
Game of Bowls, late 17th-early 18th century
10 ft. 1 in. × 15 ft. 7 in. (3 × 4.8 m)
Gift of Mr. and Mrs. Alfred J. Fisher; 52.311

Bibliography: Asselberghs 1974: 25.

Paris, Raphael de La Planche
After Simon Vouet
Adam and Eve, from the "Old Testament"
Series, mid-17th century
11 ft. 9 in. × 8 ft. 1 in. (3.6 × 2.5 m)
Gift of Mr. and Mrs. Alfred J. Fisher; 52.312

Bibliography: Fenaille 1903-23, I: 316.

Aubusson
Decorative Panel, mid-19th century
11 ft. 2 in. × 4 ft. 1 in. (3.4 × 1.2 m)
Gift of Mr. and Mrs. Harold Frank; 61.87

Beauvais Manufactory
Apollo and Daphne, ca. 1680
With the coat of arms of Vincent Hotman
and Marguerite Colbert in upper border
9 ft. 8 in. × 11 ft. 8 in. (2.9 × 3.5 m)
Gift of K.T. Keller; 62.134 See cat. no. 14

Beauvais Manufactory
Venus and Adonis, ca. 1680
With the coat of arms of Vincent
Hotman and Marguerite Colbert
in upper border
9 ft. 7 in. × 7 ft. 6 in. (2.9 × 2.2 m)
Gift of K.T. Keller; 62.136 See cat. no. 14

French or German
In the manner of David Teniers
the Younger
Scene of Country Life, early 20th century
8 ft. 7 in. × 6 ft. 6 in. (2.6 × 1.9 m)
Gift of Mrs. Herbert Weber in memory
of Mrs. Aline Weber Wright; 63.164

Aubusson
Hunting Scene, early 18th century
7 ft. 10 in. × 8 ft. 10 in. (2.3 × 2.6 m)
Gift of James S. Holden; 67.121

Gobelins Manufactory
The Child Gardeners: Autumn,
late 17th-early 18th century
10 ft. 6 in. × 8 ft. 6 in. (3.2 × 2.5 m)
Bequest of Mr. and Mrs. Lawrence P.
Fisher; 68.321

Bibliography: Fenaille 1903-23, II: 84-97,
ill. opposite p. 92.

Attributed to Aubusson
Warrior and Maiden in a Garden,
17th century
7 ft. 1 in. × 7 ft. 10 in. (2.1 × 2.3 m)
Gift of Dr. and Mrs. Harvey D. Lynn;
F82.96

Upholstery for Chair Back, ca. 1815-1835
17 in. × 13 in. (43 × 33 cm)
Gift of Bernard Savage Reilly; 1995.85

TAPESTRY-UPHOLSTERED FURNITURE

Beauvais Manufactory
Set of Tapestry Chair Covers, ca. 1785
Upholstered onto three modern *canapés*
and eight modern *fauteuils*
Canapés F71.47-F71.49: 41⅞ × 69⅜ × 32
½ in. (106.4 × 176.2 × 82.5 cm)
Fauteuils F71.50-F71.53: 39⅜ × 30½ × 26
½ in. (100 × 77.5 × 67.3 cm)
Fauteuils F71.54-F71.57: 38½ × 28½ × 26
in. (97.8 × 72.4 × 66 cm)
Bequest of Mrs. Horace E. Dodge in
memory of her husband; F71.47-F71.57

Bibliography: Dell in Dell et al. 1996:
no. 20.

Beauvais
Set of Tapestry Chair Covers, ca. 1785
Upholstered onto one modern *canapé*
and six modern *fauteuils*
Canapé F71.58: 38⅝ × 67 × 31½ in.
(98.1 × 170.2 × 80 cm)
Fauteuils F71.59-F71.64: 37½ × 25¼ ×
26⅛ in. (95.3 × 64.2 × 68.3 cm)
Bequest of Mrs. Horace E. Dodge in
memory of her husband; F71.58-F71.64

Bibliography: Dell in Dell et al. 1996:
no. 21.

GLOSSARY

AUBUSSON *(Creuse, central France)*
Family-operated tapestry workshops were active in Aubusson since the late Middle Ages. In 1665, as a means of encouraging the French tapestry industry, Jean-Baptiste Colbert, minister to Louis XIV (r. 1642–1715), issued royal letters of patent granting the Aubusson workshops the privilege of adding the title "Manufacture Royale d'Aubusson" to the weavers' monograms in the blue galloons. Throughout Aubusson's history, the private weaving enterprises never consolidated into a single manufactory, but rather continued to operate independently. An extremely prolific weaving center, Aubusson specialized in landscapes, *verdures*, and rustic genre subjects, although narrative series and copies of Gobelins and Beauvais tapestries were also woven. A revival of tapestry weaving took place in Aubusson in the 1930s and 1940s. (For a complete history, see Chevalier, Chevalier, and Bertrand 1988.)

BEAUVAIS MANUFACTORY *(Oise, northern France).*
Although established as a royal manufactory in 1664, the Beauvais manufactory was a private enterprise, dependent on individual commissions for its revenue. Unlike the Gobelins, Beauvais catered primarily to an aristocratic clientele rather than the Crown and consequently remained a commercial operation throughout its history. The manufactory suffered precarious financial health under its first four directors, despite some early successes such as the "Grotesques" series, introduced in the late seventeenth century under the Tournai weaver Philippe Béhagle (1684–1705). By the early eighteenth century, Beauvais rivaled the Gobelins and Brussels workshops in the quality of weaving and design. Fresh new cartoons provided by artistic director Jean-Baptiste Oudry from the mid-1720s and by François Boucher beginning in 1735 reflected the fashionable new rococo taste and met with commercial and critical acclaim. A state-owned concern since 1794, Beauvais merged with the Gobelins manufactory in 1940. (For a complete history, see Badin 1909 and Coural and Gastinel-Coural 1992.)

BORDER
A decorative band, of varying width and design, framing the tapestry. Introduced as a decorative element around 1480, borders are often characteristic of a specific factory, workshop, or weaving center during a certain period and can be useful in dating the tapestry.

CARTOON
A finished, full-scale drawing of the tapestry, executed either in black-and-white or color, on scored paper or canvas. Using the cartoon as the guide, the weaver traces its outlines onto the tensioned warp with dark ink. These outlines indicate where the weft color changes as the weft threads are woven into the warp. The cartoon remains in place behind the high-warp loom (the weaver sees the cartoon's reflection in a mirror set up in front of him or her) or beneath the warp of a low-warp loom during the weaving process.

CHINOISERIE
An exotic and often whimsical style of decoration that freely imitated Asian art and design, especially that of China and Japan. Although *chinoiserie* appeared in Europe centuries earlier with the advent of the Asian trade, it reached its height of popularity in the eighteenth century.

ENTREFENÊTRE
A narrow tapestry panel, generally intended to hang between two windows.

GALLOON

The plain, narrow outer border of the tapestry, sometimes woven with the mark of the factory or weaver. The galloon protects the tapestry at its edges and gives strength to the hanging. Also called a guard or a *galon*.

GOBELINS MANUFACTORY (*Paris*)

The most important French tapestry factory of the late seventeenth and eighteenth centuries, the royal Gobelins manufactory was established in Paris by Jean-Baptiste Colbert, Louis XIV's minister, in 1662. The Gobelins initially produced all manner of luxury furnishings for the royal residences, including furniture, silver, and bronzes. In 1694, a financial crisis precipitated by the War of the League of Augsburg caused the temporary closure of the factory. After reopening in 1699, the factory produced tapestry exclusively, providing the Crown with hangings for its own use and as diplomatic gifts. A dramatic reorganization of the factory's administration in the early eighteenth century placed an artist in charge of the design workshop for the first time. The artistic directors—who included François Boucher (1755–70)—led the factory away from the heroic narratives favored during the late seventeenth century and toward more decorative series which became luxurious alternatives to oil painting, complete with simulated gilded frames. During the eighteenth century the Gobelins commissioned cartoons from prominent French painters while refining the art of tapestry weaving to its highest degree. A state manufactory since 1794, the Gobelins continues in production today. (For a complete history, see Coural 1989 and Fenaille 1903–23.)

HIGH-WARP LOOM

A tapestry loom having the parallel warp threads stretched vertically between top and bottom rollers. Traditionally, the weaver works from the back of the tapestry, following the cartoon placed behind him and seen in reverse in a mirror. Also called *haute-lisse*, this type of loom was used in the workshops of the southern Netherlands, at the Gobelins Manufactory in Paris, and by Morris and Company at Merton Abbey in England.

LOW-WARP LOOM

A tapestry loom with the parallel warp threads stretched in a horizontal position. The weaver operates the loom by means of foot pedals and works from the cartoon placed beneath the warp threads. Also called *basse-lisse*, the low-warp loom was used at the Gobelins Manufactory in Paris and in Aubusson. Because the weaver can operate the loom using both his or her hands and feet, the textile production is faster and therefore less expensive than on a high-warp loom.

MERTON ABBEY TAPESTRY WORKS (*Surrey, England*)

William Morris revived the art of tapestry weaving in England at Merton Abbey in 1881. Morris had established a firm in London in 1861 for the production of decorative articles for the home. Reorganized as Morris and Company in 1875, the successful firm moved in 1881 to Merton Abbey, where Morris set up looms for tapestry weaving. Merton Abbey specialized in richly colored and ornately patterned tapestries, inspired by late medieval Netherlandish precedents and often depicting subjects taken from medieval literature. In addition, weavers employed the traditional techniques and materials of the medieval Flemish workshops, including vegetal-dyed wools and high-warp looms. The firm's chief designer, painter Edward Burne-Jones, provided the majority of cartoons for the figurative tapestries until his death in 1898. Merton Abbey suffered financial difficulties during the World War I and closed in 1940. (For a complete history, see Marillier 1927 and Parry 1983.)

METALLIC THREAD

Extremely thin sheets of metal, generally gold or silver, are wrapped around a core of another material, such as silk, to produce metallic thread. Used for only the weft of the most sumptuous weavings, metallic threads highlight principal figures or elements in the design.

MILLEFLEURS

A tapestry with a decorative background filled entirely with scattered flowers and plants. Figures, animals, heraldic emblems, and other devices may stand out against the dense background having little or no illusion of spatial depth. The most common ground color is dark blue, although other colors, including red, were also used.

PETIT PATRON

A small-scale, finished drawing for a tapestry design, from which the cartoon is made.

TAPESTRY

For the purpose of this exhibition, tapestry is defined as a textile structure having one warp and a weft composed of differently colored threads that do not pass from edge to edge but are interwoven only with the part of the warp that is required for a particular pattern area. As they are interwoven across the width of the tapestry, the weft threads are packed down onto the warp by means of a comb, so that they completely cover the warp. These discontinuous weft threads form the pattern.

VERDURE

A decorative tapestry depicting primarily green forests, leaves, and fruit, and occasionally including animals or small-scale human figures. This term does not apply to tapestries with predominant figures or architectural elements or those emphasizing a narrative scene.

WARP

The threads of the tapestry (most commonly of undyed wool) that are set up parallel to one another on the loom prior to weaving and are held taut by the loom's beams.

WEFT

The transverse threads that are interwoven with the warp, under one thread and over the next, by means of a bobbin.

BIBLIOGRAPHY

ACKERMAN 1932
Ackerman, Phyllis. *The Rockefeller McCormick Tapestries: Three Early Sixteenth Century Tapestries.* New York, 1932.

ACKERMAN 1940
————. "Early Flemish Tapestries in the Collection of William Randolph Hearst, Esq." *The Connoisseur* 105 (June 1940): 187–194.

ADELAIDE 1994
Adelaide, the Art Gallery of South Australia. *Morris and Company: Pre-Raphaelites and the Arts and Crafts Movement in South Australia.* Catalogue by Christopher Menz. Exhibition, 1994.

ADELSON 1994
Adelson, Candace J. *European Tapestry in The Minneapolis Institute of Arts.* Minneapolis, 1994.

ANANOFF AND WILDENSTEIN 1976
Ananoff, Alexandre, and Daniel Wildenstein. *François Boucher.* 2 vols. Lausanne and Paris, 1976.

ANTIQUES 1978
"Textiles in Detroit." *The Magazine Antiques* 114 (September 1978): 392.

ARRAS 1988
Arras, Musée des Beaux-Arts, and Musée Departmental de la Tapisserie, Aubusson. *Jeux et divertissements: Tapisseries du XVIe au XVIIIe siècle.* Exhibition, 1988.

ART JOURNAL 1908
"Noteworthy Handicrafts." *The Art Journal* (1908): 182.

ART QUARTERLY 1957
"Recent Important Acquisitions of American Collections." *The Art Quarterly* 20 (summer 1957): 217–29.

ART QUARTERLY 1971
"Recent Acquisitions of American and Canadian Museums." *The Art Quarterly* 34 (winter 1971): 494–508.

ASSELBERGHS 1974
Asselberghs, Jean-Paul. *Les tapisseries flamandes aux Etats-Unis d'Amérique.* Brussels, 1974.

ASSELBERGHS, DELMARCEL, AND GARCIA CALVO 1985
Asselberghs, Jean-Paul, Guy Delmarcel, and Margarita Garcia Calvo. "Un tapissier bruxellois actif en Espagne: François Tons." *Bulletin des Musées Royaux d'Art et d'Histoire, Bruxelles* 56 (1985): 89–121.

BADIN 1909
Badin, Jules. *La manufacture de tapisseries de Beauvais.* Paris, 1909.

BALDASS 1924
Baldass, Ludwig von. "Masterpieces of the Art of Flemish Tapestry-Weaving." *Bulletin of the Bachstitz Gallery,* The Hague and New York, 7/8 (September 1924): 2–6.

BALDASS 1924A
————. "Die Paulustapisserien des Pieter Coecke van Alost." *Belvedere* 5 (January-July 1924): 45–49.

BENNETT 1992
Bennett, Anna Gray. *Five Centuries of Tapestry from The Fine Arts Museums of San Francisco.* San Francisco, 1992.

BÖTTIGER 1928
Böttiger, John. *Tapisseries à figures des XVIe et XVIIe siècles appartenant à des collections privées de la Suède.* Stockholm, 1928.

BOYCE 1910
Boyce, Cecil. "The British Losses at the Brussels Exhibition." *The Connoiseur* 28 (October 1910): 138.

BROWN 1996
Brown, Clifford M., and Guy Delmarcel. *Tapestries for the Courts of Federico II, Ercole, and Ferrante Gonzaga, 1522-63.* Seattle, 1996.

BRUGES 1960
Bruges, Musée Groeninge. *Le siècle des primitifs flamands.* Exhibition, 1960.

BRUGES 1987
Bruges, Gruuthusemuseum. *Bruges et la tapisserie.* Catalogue by Guy Delmarcel and Erik Duverger. Exhibition, 1987.

BRUSSELS 1947
Brussels, Palais des Beaux-Arts. *La tapisserie française du moyen âge à nos jours.* Catalogue introduction by Pierre Verlet. Exhibition, 1947.

BRUSSELS 1976
Brussels, Musées royaux d'art et d'histoire. *Tapisseries bruxelloises de la pré-Renaissance.* Catalogue by Guy Delmarcel. Exhibition, 1976.

BRUSSELS 1977
————. *Tapisseries bruxelloises au siècle de Rubens.* Catalogue by Rotrand Bauer and Guy Delmarcel. Exhibition, 1977.

BURNE-JONES 1900
Burne-Jones, Philip. "Notes on Some Unfinished Work of Sir Edward Burne-Jones." *The Magazine of Art* 23 (1900): 159–67.

CAMPBELL 1994
Campbell, Thomas. Review of *Medieval Tapestries in The Metropolitan Museum of Art* by Adolfo Cavallo, in *Burlington Magazine* 136 (December 1994): 842–43.

CAMPBELL 1995
————. "Tapestry Quality for Tudor England: Problems of Terminology." *Studies in the Decorative Arts* 3 (fall-winter 1995–96): 29–50.

CAVALLO 1952
Cavallo, Adolph S. "The Procession of Gula, A Flemish Tapestry." *Bulletin of the Detroit Institute of Arts* 32 (1952–53): 86–89.

CAVALLO 1967
_____. *Tapestries of Europe and of Colonial Peru in the Museum of Fine Arts, Boston.* 2 vols. Boston, 1967.

CAVALLO 1979
_____. "The Garden of Vanity: A Millefleurs Tapestry." *Bulletin of the Detroit Institute of Arts* 57 (1979): 30–39.

CAVALLO 1993
_____. *Medieval Tapestries in The Metropolitan Museum of Art.* New York, 1993.

CHEVALIER, CHEVALIER, AND BERTRAND 1988
Chevalier, Dominique, Pierre Chevalier, and Pascal-François Bertrand. *Les tapisseries d'Aubusson et de Felletin, 1457-1791.* Paris, 1988.

CLEVELAND 1966
Cleveland, The Cleveland Museum of Art. *Treasures from Medieval France.* Catalogue by William Wixom. Exhibition, 1966-67.

COURAL 1989
Coural, Jean. *Les Gobelins.* Paris, 1989.

COURAL AND GASTINEL-COURAL 1992
Coural, Jean, and Chantal Gastinel-Coural. *Beauvais, Manufacture nationale de tapisserie.* Paris, 1992.

DE LA CHENAYE-DESBOIS AND BADIER 1864
De la Chenaye-Desbois and Badier. *Dictionnaire de la noblesse.* Paris, 1864.

DELL ET AL. 1996
Dell, Theodore, et al. *The Dodge Collection of Eighteenth-Century French and English Art at The Detroit Institute of Arts.* New York and Detroit, 1996.

DELMARCEL 1979
Delmarcel, Guy. "'The Triumph of the Seven Virtues' and Related Brussels Tapestries of the Early Renaissance." *Acts of the Tapestry Symposium, November 1976,* pp. 155–70. San Francisco, 1979.

DEMOTTE 1924
Demotte, G.J. *La Tapisserie gothique.* Paris, 1924.

DETROIT 1928
Detroit, The Detroit Institute of Arts. *Seventh Loan Exhibition: French Gothic Art of the Thirteenth to Fifteenth Century.* Exhibition, 1928.

DETROIT 1933
_____. *A Catalogue of Works of Art in the Collection of Anna Thomson Dodge.* Detroit, 1933.

DETROIT 1939
_____. *A Catalogue of Works of Art of the Eighteenth Century in the Collection of Anna Thomson Dodge.* 2 vols. Detroit, 1939.

DETROIT 1942
_____. "The Arts Commission Annual Report for the year 1941." *Bulletin of the Detroit Institute of Arts* 21: 37, 44; February 1942.

DETROIT 1945
_____. *Four Hundred Years of Tapestries.* Checklist by Adele Coulin Weibel. Exhibition, 1945.

DETROIT 1958
_____. *Decorative Arts of the Italian Renaissance 1400-1600.* Exhibition, 1958–59.

DETROIT 1960
_____. *Masterpieces of Flemish Art: van Eyck to Bosch.* Exhibition, 1960.

DETROIT 1971
_____. *The Detroit Institute of Arts Illustrated Handbook.* Detroit, 1971.

DETROIT 1976
_____. *Arts and Crafts in Detroit.* Catalogue by Sheila K. Tabakoff et al. Exhibition, 1976–77.

DETROIT 1978
_____. *Textile Masterpieces from the Detroit Institute of Arts.* Guide by Adolfo Cavallo et al. Exhibition, 1978–79.

DETROIT 1982
_____. *Selected Renaissance Works of Art from the Permanent Collection.* Guide by Alan Darr et al. Exhibition, 1982–83.

DETROIT 1984
_____. *The Art of Chivalry: European Arms and Armor from The Metropolitan Museum of Art.* Exhibition, 1984.

DETROIT 1991
_____. *Clothed in Majesty: European Ecclesiastical Textiles from the Detroit Institute of Arts.* Catalogue by Peter Barnet. Exhibition, 1991–92.

DETROIT 1993
_____. *Decorative Arts 1900: Highlights from Private Collections in Detroit.* Catalogue by Peter Barnet and MaryAnn Wilkinson. Exhibition, 1993–94.

DETROIT 1995
_____. *The Detroit Institute of Arts: A Visitor's Guide.* Edited by Julia P. Henshaw, 1995.

DIDEROT 1771
Diderot, Denis, ed. *L'Encyclopédie, Recueil de planches sur les sciences, les arts libéraux, et les arts méchaniciens,* vol. IX. Paris, 1771.

DUVERGER 1959
Duverger, J. "De Rijschool of Grote en Kleine Paarden in de XVIIe eeuwse Tapijtkunst." *La tapisserie flamande aux XVII et XVIII siècles (International Colloquium).* pp. 163–65. Brussels, 1959.

DUVERGER 1969
Duverger, Erik. "Tapijtwerk uit het atelier van Frans Geubels." *De bloeitijd van de Vlaamse tapijtkunst.* pp. 174–78. Brussels, 1969.

FAIRCLOUGH AND LEARY 1981
Fairclough, Oliver, and Emmeline Leary. *Textiles by William Morris and Morris & Co., 1861-1940.* London, 1981.

FENAILLE 1903-23
Fenaille, Maurice. *Etat général des tapisseries de la manufacture des Gobelins depuis l'origine jusqu'à nos jours 1600-1900.* 5 vols. Paris, 1903–23.

FORTI GRAZZINI 1982
Forti Grazzini, Nello. *L'arazzo ferrarese.* Milan, 1982.

FORTI GRAZZINI 1993
_____. *Il patrimonio artistico del Quirinale: Gli arazzi.* 2 vols. Rome and Milan, 1993.

FRIEDLÄNDER 1917
Friedländer, M.J. "Pieter Coecke van Alost." *Jahrbuch der Königlich Preuszischen Kunstsammlungen* 38 (1917): 73–94.

GAZETTE DES BEAUX-ARTS 1972
"La chronique des arts." *Gazette des Beaux-Arts* 79 (February 1972): supplement, 1–88.

GÖBEL 1923
Göbel, Heinrich. *Wandteppiche, I: Die Niederlande.* 2 vols. Leipzig, 1923.

GÖBEL 1928
_____. *Wandteppiche, II: Die Romanischen Länder.* 2 vols. Leipzig, 1928.

GÖBEL 1934
_____. *Wandteppiche, III: Die Germanischen und Slawischen Länder.* 2 vols. Berlin, 1934.

GRAND RAPIDS 1956
Grand Rapids, Grand Rapids Art Gallery. *Christmas Exhibition.* Exhibition, 1956–57.

GRUBER 1992
Gruber, Alain, ed. *L'art décoratif en Europe, II: Classique et baroque.* Paris, 1992.

GUIFFREY 1885
Guiffrey, Jules. *Inventaire général du mobilier de la couronne sous Louis XIV (1663-1715).* 2 vols. Paris, 1885.

HARTFORD 1951
Hartford, Wadsworth Atheneum, and Baltimore Museum of Art, Baltimore. *Two Thousand Years of Tapestry Weaving.* Exhibition, 1951–52.

HEFFORD 1983
Hefford, Wendy. "The Chicago Pygmalion and the 'English Metamorphoses'." *The Art Institute of Chicago Centennial Lectures (Museum Studies 10).* pp. 93–116. Chicago, 1983.

HIESINGER 1976
Hiesinger, Kathryn B. "The Sources of François Boucher's Psyche Tapestries." *Bulletin of the Philadelphia Museum of Art* 62 (November 1976): 7–23.

HOLLSTEIN N.D.
Hollstein, F.W.H. *Dutch and Flemish Etchings, Engravings, and Woodcuts, ca. 1450-1700.* Vol. 13. Amsterdam, n.d.

JESTAZ 1977
Jestaz, Bernard. "La manufacture de Beauvais sous la direction de Béhagle: Documents inédits." *Bulletin de la Société de l'Histoire de l'Art Français* (1977): 145–51.

JESTAZ 1979
_____. "The Beauvais Manufactory in 1690." *Acts of the Tapestry Symposium, November 1976,* pp. 187–208. San Francisco, 1979.

JOUBERT, LEFÉBURE, AND BERTRAND 1995
Joubert, Fabienne, Amaury Lefébure, and Pascal-François Bertrand. *Histoire de la tapisserie en Europe, du Moyen Âge à nos jours.* Paris, 1995.

KATONAH 1992
Katonah, New York, Katonah Museum of Art. *Designing Utopia: The Art of William Morris and His Circle.* Exhibition, 1992.

KNOWLTON 1956
Knowlton, Edgar C. "The Scale of Man." *Studies in the Renaissance* 3 (1956):131–44.

LANGER AND OTTOMEYER 1995
Langer, Brigitte, and Hans Ottomeyer. *Die Möbel der Residenz München,* vol. 1, *Die französischen Möbel des 18. Jahrhunderts.* Munich and New York, 1995.

LAPEYRE AND SCHEURER 1978
Lapeyre, André, and Rémy Scheurer. *Les notaires et secrétaires du roi sous les règnes de Louis XI, Charles VIII et Louis XII (1461-1515).* Vol. 1. Paris, 1978.

LAUSANNE 1995
Lausanne, Bâtiment du Grand Conseil. *Tapisseries de Bruges, Bruxelles et Beauvais, XVIIe et XVIIIe siècles. Chefs-d'oeuvre de la collection Toms.* Catalogue by Nicole de Reyniès, Guy Delmarcel, and Philippe Lüscher. Exhibition, 1995.

LEDOUX-LEBARD 1975
Ledoux-Lebard, Denise. *Inventaire général du Musée National de Versailles et des Trianons.* Vol. 1, *Le Grand Trianon: Meubles et objets d'art.* Paris, 1975.

LONDON 1888
London. *Arts and Crafts Society Exhibition.* Essay by William Morris. Exhibition, 1888.

LONDON 1912
Lord Michelham: Catalogue of Works of Art. London, 1912.

LONDON 1938
London, Christie's. *Fine Decorative Furniture Important Objects of Art, Tapestry, Sculpture and Rugs Being a Part of the Collection Formed by the Late Mortimer L. Schiff, Esq.* Sale cat., June 22–23, 1938.

LONDON 1996
London, Victoria and Albert Museum. *William Morris.* Linda Parry, ed. Exhibition, 1996.

LUNDGREN 1979
Lundgren, Harold P. "Tapestry Wools, Ancient to Modern." *Acts of the Tapestry Symposium, November 1976,* pp. 21–27. San Francisco. 1979.

MACFALL 1908
Macfall, Haldane. *Boucher: The Man, His Times, His Art, and His Significance.* London, 1908.

MARILIER 1966
Marilier, Georges. *La renaissance flamande: Pierre Coeck d'Alost.* Brussels, 1966.

MARILLIER 1927
Marillier, H.C. *History of the Merton Abbey Tapestry Works.* London, 1927.

MARILLIER 1930
_____. *English Tapestries of the 18th Century.* London, 1930.

MASSCHELEIN-KLEINER 1979
Masschelein-Kleiner, Liliane. "Dyeing Techniques of Tapestries in the Southern Netherlands During the Fifteenth and Sixteenth Centuries." *Acts of the Tapestry Symposium, November 1976,* pp. 29–40. San Francisco. 1979.

MIGEON 1909
Migeon, Gaston. "Collection de M. Ch. Mège." *Les Arts* 86 (February 1909):2–18.

MOLINIER 1902
Molinier, Émile. "Le mobilier français du XVIIIe siècle." *Les Arts* 1 (January 1902): 19–23.

MONACO 1991
Monaco, Sotheby's. *Bel ameublement.* Sale cat., June 22–23, 1991.

MÜNTZ 1878–84
Müntz, Eugène. *Histoire de la tapisserie en Italie, en Allemagne, en Angleterre, en Espagne, en Danemark, en Hongrie, en Pologne, en Russie, et en Turquie.* Vol. 2. Paris, 1878-1884.

Müntz 1902
_____. "Tapisseries allégoriques inédites ou peu connues." *Commission de la Fondation Eugène Piot. Monuments et mémoires* 9 (1902): 95–121.

New York 1915
New York, American Art Association. *Costly Art Property from the Collection of the Duc D'Avaray of Paris.* Sale cat., January 22–23, 1915.

New York 1923
New York, The Anderson Galleries. *The Henry Symons Collections.* Sale cat., January 27-February 3, 1923.

New York 1949
New York, Parke-Bernet. *French Furniture, Tapestries, Objets d'Art.* Sale cat., January 28–29, 1949.

New York 1974
New York, The Metropolitan Museum of Art. *Masterpieces of Tapestry from the Fourteenth to the Sixteenth Century.* Catalogue by Geneviéve Souchal. Exhibition 1974.

Packer 1961
Packer, Charles. "French Tapestry Chair Coverings." *The Connoisseur* 147 (April 1961): 141–47.

Paden 1995
Paden, William D. "Pastourelle/Pastorela." *Medieval France. An Encyclopedia.* Edited by William W. Kibler and Grover A. Zinn. New York and London, 1995.

Pallot 1993
Pallot, Bill G.B. *Furniture Collections in the Louvre.* Vol. 2, *Chairs and Consoles (Menuiserie), 17th and 18th Centuries.* Dijon, 1993.

Paris 1880
Paris, Musée des Arts Décoratifs. *Catalogue descriptif des tapisseries exposées au Musée des Arts Décoratifs en 1880.* Exhibition, 1880.

Paris 1905
Pris, Galerie Georges Petit. *Catalogue des tableaux…composant la Collection de M. E. Cronier.* Sale cat., December 4–5, 1905.

Paris 1923
Paris, Galerie Georges Petit. *[Madame Billout-Desmarets Collection].* Sale cat., June 1, 1923.

Paris 1928
Paris, Musée de la Manufacture Nationale des Gobelins. *La tapisserie gothique.* Exhibition, 1928.

Paris 1973
Paris, Grand Palais. *Chefs d'oeuvre de la tapisserie du XIVe au XVIe siècle.* Exhibition, 1973–74.

Paris 1978
_____. *Jules Romain, L'Histoire de Scipion: tapisseries et dessins.* Catalogue by Bernard Jestaz and Roseline Bacou. Exhibition, 1978.

Parry 1975
Parry, Linda. "The Tapestries of Edward Burne-Jones." *Apollo* 102 (November 1975): 324–28.

Parry 1983
_____. *William Morris Textiles.* New York, 1983.

Parry 1983A
_____. "The Revival of the Merton Abbey Tapestry Works." *The Journal of the William Morris Society* 5 (1983): 16–22.

Paris 1985
Paris, Musée du Louvre. *Nouvelles acquisitions du département des Objets d'art 1980-1984.* Exhibition, 1985.

Peck 1991
Peck, William. *The Detroit Institute of Arts: A Brief History.* Detroit, 1991.

Pittsburgh 1987
Pittsburgh, The Frick Art Museum. *Old Master Drawings from Chatsworth: A Loan Exhibition from the Devonshire Collection.* Catalogue by Michael Jaffé. Exhibition organized by the International Exhibitions Foundation, Alexandria, Virginia, 1987–88.

Pochat 1973
Pochat, G. "Triumphus Regis Gosci sive Gutschmin. Exoticism in French Renaissance Tapestry." *Gazette des Beaux-Arts* 6e pér., LXXXII (1973): 305–10.

Providence 1979
Providence, Rhode Island School of Design, and The Cooper-Hewitt Museum, New York. *Fantastic Illustration and Design in Britain 1850-1930.* Catalogue by Diana L. Johnson. Exhibition, 1979.

Raynor 1992
Raynor, Vivian. "Designs by William Morris and His Circle of Utopian Artists." *The New York Times* (March 8, 1992).

Reyniès 1995
Reyniès, Nicole de. "Jean van Orley: Une tenture de l'Histoire de Psyché." *Gazette des Beaux-Arts* 125 (March 1995): 208–20.

Sánchez Beltrán 1983
Sánchez Beltrán, Maria Jesús. "Los Tapices del Museo Arqueológico Nacional." *Boletin del Museo Arqueológico Nacional* 1 (1983): 47–82.

Schloss Halbturn 1981
Austria, Schloss Halbturn. *Tapisserien der Renaissance nach Entwurfen von Pieter Coecke von Aelst.* Catalogue by Rotrand Bauer. Exhibition, 1981.

Seelig 1976
Seelig, Lorenz. "Gothic and Early Renaissance Tapestries." *The Connoisseur* (September 1976): 26–33.

Shearman 1972
Shearman, John. *Raphael's Cartoons in the Collection of Her Majesty the Queen and the Tapestries for the Sistine Chapel.* London, 1971.

Shepherd 1961
Shepherd, Dorothy G. "Three Tapestries from Chaumont." *Bulletin of the Cleveland Museum of Art* 48 (September 1961): 158–77.

Souchal 1979
Souchal, Geneviève. "'The Triumph of the Seven Virtues': Reconstruction of a Brussels Series (ca. 1520-1535)." *Acts of the Tapestry Symposium, November 1976,* pp.103–53. San Francisco, 1979.

Standen 1964
Standen, Edith A. "The 'Sujets de la Fable' Gobelins Tapestries." *The Art Bulletin* 46 (June 1964): 43-57.

STANDEN 1971
_____. "Drawings for the Months of Lucas Tapestry Series." *Master Drawings* 9 (Spring 1971): 3-14.

STANDEN 1979
_____. "Some Beauvais Tapestries Related to Bérain." *Acts of the Tapestry Symposium, November 1976*, pp. 209-13. San Francisco, 1979.

STANDEN 1981
_____. "Studies in the History of Tapestry 1520-1790." *Apollo* (July 1981): 6-54.

STANDEN 1981A
_____. "Tapestries in the Collection of the Museum of Art, Carnegie Institute." *Carnegie Magazine* 55 (December 1981): 2-7.

STANDEN 1985
_____. *European Post-Medieval Tapestries and Related Hangings in The Metropolitan Museum of Art.* 2 vols. New York, 1985.

STANDEN 1987
_____. "Renaissance to Modern Tapestries in The Metropolitan Museum of Art." Reprinted from *The Metropolitan Museum of Art Bulletin* (spring 1987).

STANDEN 1994
_____. "Country Children: Some 'Enfants de Boucher' in Gobelins Tapestry." *Metropolitan Museum Journal* 29 (1994): 111-33.

STERLING 1966
Sterling, Charles. "La Pieta de Tarascon et les peintres Dombet." *La Revue du Louvre et des Musées de France* 16 (1966): 13-26.

STERNE 1980
Sterne, Margaret. *The Passionate Eye: The Life of William R. Valentiner.* Detroit, 1980.

THOMAS 1990
Thomas, Laurent. *Les tapisseries des mois de Lucas.* 2 vols. Master's thesis (unpublished), Université de Paris, 1990-1991.

THURMAN 1979
Thurman, Christa C. M. "Tapestry: The Purposes, Form, and Function of the Medium from Its Inception until Today." *Acts of the Tapestry Symposium, November 1976*, pp. 3-19. San Francisco, 1979.

THURMAN 1992
_____. *Textiles in the Art Institute of Chicago.* Chicago, 1992.

THE TIMES 1923
"A Merton Abbey Tapestry for America." *The Times,* London (December 23, 1923).

TOURNAI 1970
Tournai, Cathedral of Nôtre-Dame. *Tapisseries héraldiques et de la vie quotidienne des XVe et XVIe siècles.* Exhibition, 1970.

T.R. 1908
T.R. "The Craft Section at the New Gallery." *The Studio* 44 (1908): 55-62.

VALLANCE 1908
Vallance, Aymer. "Some Examples of Tapestry Designed by Sir E. Burne Jones and Mr. J.H. Dearle." *The Studio* 45 (1908): 13-24.

VERSAILLES 1967
Versailles, Orangerie. *Chefs-d'oeuvre de la tapisserie parisienne, 1597-1662.* Exhibition, 1967.

VIALLET 1971
Viallet, Nicole. *Tapisserie, méthode et vocabularie.* Paris, 1971.

VIANDEN 1995
Luxembourg, Château de Vianden. *Flemish Tapestries: Five Centuries of Tradition.* Catalogue by Guy Delmarcel and An Volckaert. Exhibition, 1995.

WALTHER 1924
Walther, J[osephine]. "Flemish Tapestries." *Bulletin of the Detroit Institute of Arts* 6 (October 1924): 4-6.

WARD 1953
Ward, Evelyn Svec. "Four Seasons Tapestries from Gobelins." *Bulletin of the Cleveland Museum of Art* 40 (June 1953): 113-19.

WATSON 1961
Watson, F.J.B. "French Tapestry Chair Coverings: A Popular Fallacy Re-examined." *The Connoisseur* 148 (October 1961): 166-69.

WEIBEL 1927
Weibel, Adele Coulin. "The Passing of Venus." *Bulletin of the Detroit Institute of Arts* 8 (1927): 78-80.

WEIBEL 1932
_____. "Recent Gifts to the Textile Department." *Bulletin of the Detroit Institute of Arts* 13 (May 1932): 99-102.

WEIBEL 1935
_____. "Tapestries by Peeter Wauters." *Bulletin of the Detroit Institute of Arts* 14 (January 1935): 44-47.

WEIBEL 1935A
_____. "Eros Triumphant." *Bulletin of the Detroit Institute of Arts* 14 (March 1935): 76-81.

WEIBEL 1943
_____. "A Late Gothic Tapestry." *Bulletin of the Detroit Institute of Arts* 22 (May 1943): 79-81.

WEIBEL 1947
_____. "A Fragment of a Gobelin Border." *Bulletin of the Detroit Institute of Arts* 26 (1947): 62.

WEIBEL 1947A
_____. "Tapestries by Franz and Jacob Geubels." *Bulletin of the Detroit Institute of Arts* 27 (1947): 6-10.

WEIBEL 1950
_____. "An Early Gobelins Tapestry." *Bulletin of the Detroit Institute of Arts* 30 (1950-51): 4-7.

WEIBEL 1956
_____. "An Oudenarde Tapestry." *Bulletin of the Detroit Institute of Arts* 36 (1956-57): 12-13.

WEIBEL 1957
_____. "A Millefleurs Tapestry." *Bulletin of the Detroit Institute of Arts* 36 (1957): 89-90.

WEIBEL 1959
————. "A Pair of Franco-Flemish Tapestries." *Bulletin of the Detroit Institute of Arts* 39 (1959–60): 96–97.

WEIBEL AND ROBINSON 1955
Weibel, Adele Coulin, and Francis W. Robinson. *Four Late Gothic Flemish Tapestries of Virtues and Vices from the Collection of William Randolph Hearst.* Detroit, 1955.

WEIBEL AND ROBINSON 1956
————. "Four Late Gothic Allegorical Tapestries." *Bulletin of the Detroit Institute of Arts* 36 (1956–57): 60–63.

WELLS 1959
Wells, William. "Family Pride." *Scottish Art Review* 7 (1959): 14–16, 28.

WILMINGTON 1976
Wilmington, Art Museum. *The Pre-Raphaelite Era, 1848-1914.* Catalogue by Rowland and Betty Elzea. Exhibition, 1976.

WINOKUR 1971
Winokur, Ronald L. "The Mr. and Mrs. Horace E. Dodge Memorial Collection." *Bulletin of The Detroit Institute of Arts* 50 (1971): 43–51.

WIXOM 1961
Wixom, William D. "Traditions in the Chaumont Tapestries." *The Bulletin of the Cleveland Museum of Art* 44 (September 1961): 182–89.

WORCESTER 1969
Worcester, Worcester Art Museum. *The Virtuoso Craftsman: Northern European Design in the 16th Century.* Exhibition, 1969.

YPERSELE DE STRIHOU 1970
Ypersele de Strihou, A., and P. van. *Laeken.* Brussels, 1970.

ZICK 1972
Zick, Gisela. "Der Triumph der Liebe, zur Quellen- und Motivgeschichte eines Bildteppichs nach Edward Burne-Jones." *Wallraf-Richartz-Jahrbuch* 34 (1972): 307–48.

Index

DESIGN
Hammond Design, Ann Arbor, Michigan

PRINTING
Grigg Graphic Services, Inc.
Southfield, Michigan

COLOR SEPARATIONS
Silva Graphics USA, Southfield, Michigan

TYPOGRAPHY
Minion and Minion Expert Series

PAPER
100 LB Centura Gloss Cover
80 LB Warren Patina Text